The city of Rome is bu   ...arble but also of the
words of its writers. Fo.... ancient inhabitant or visitor, the buildings
of Rome, the public spaces of the city, were crowded with meanings
and associations. These meanings were generated partly through
activities associated with particular places, but Rome also took on
meanings from literature written about the city: stories of its foundation,
praise of its splendid buildings, laments composed by those obliged to
leave it. Ancient writers made use of the city to explore the complexities
of Roman history, power and identity. This book aims to chart
selected aspects of Rome's resonance in literature and the literary
resonance of Rome. A wide range of texts are explored, from later
periods as well as from antiquity, since, as the author hopes to show,
Gibbon, Goethe, and others can be revealing guides to the literary
topography of ancient Rome.

ROMAN LITERATURE
AND ITS CONTEXTS

Writing Rome

ROMAN LITERATURE
AND ITS CONTEXTS

Series editors
Denis Feeney and Stephen Hinds

This series promotes approaches to Roman literature which are open to dialogue with current work in other areas of the classics, and in the humanities at large. The pursuit of contacts with cognate fields such as social history, anthropology, history of thought, linguistics and literary theory is in the best traditions of classical scholarship: the study of Roman literature, no less than Greek, has much to gain from engaging with these other contexts and intellectual traditions. The series offers a forum in which readers of Latin texts can sharpen their readings by placing them in broader and better-defined contexts, and in which other classicists and humanists can explore the general or particular implications of their work for readers of Latin texts. The books all constitute original and innovative research and are envisaged as suggestive essays whose aim is to stimulate debate.

Other books in the series

Philip Hardie, *The epic successors of Virgil: a study in the dynamics of a tradition*

Duncan F. Kennedy, *The arts of love: five studies in the discourse of Roman love elegy*

Charles Martindale, *Redeeming the text: Latin poetry and the hermeneutics of reception*

Writing Rome

Textual approaches
to the city

Catharine Edwards

*Senior Research Fellow (Leverhulme Project),
Department of Classics and Ancient History,
University of Bristol*

CAMBRIDGE
UNIVERSITY PRESS

Published by the Press Syndicate of the University of Cambridge
The Pitt Building, Trumpington Street, Cambridge CB2 1RP
40 West 20th Street, New York, NY 10011-4211, USA
10 Stamford Road, Oakleigh, Melbourne 3166, Australia

First published 1996

A catalogue record for this book is available from the British Library

Library of Congress cataloguing in publication data
Edwards, Catharine.
Writing Rome: textual approaches to the city/Catharine Edwards.
p.   cm. – (Roman literature and its contexts)
Includes bibliographical references and index.
ISBN 0 521 55080 7 (hardback). – ISBN 0 521 55952 9 (paperback)
1. Latin literature – History and criticism. 2. Literature, Modern –
Roman influences. 3. City and town life in literature.
4. Cities and towns in literature. 5. Literature and society – Rome.
6. Rome (Italy) – In literature. 7. Rome – In literature. I. Title.
II. Series.
PA6019.E39   1996
870.9′321732–dc20   95-52327   CIP

ISBN 0 521 55080 7 hardback
ISBN 0 521 55952 9 paperback

Transferred to digital printing 2000

vestigia etiam nunc manent.
Varro

Contents

Plates

(between pages 26 and 27)

1 'The artist's despair before the grandeur of ancient ruins', Henry
Fuseli c. 1778/80 © 1995, Copyright by Kunsthaus Zurich. All rights
reserved.

2 'Scenographia' from *Il Campo Marzio dell' Antica Roma*, G. B.
Piranesi, 1762. Arch. Ba3. By courtesy of the Bodleian Library,
University of Oxford.

3 Plan of Rome from *Antichità Romane de' Tempi della Repubblica e de'
Primi Imperatori*, G. B. Piranesi, 1748. By courtesy of the University
Library, Cambridge.

4 Mussolini addressing young Fascists on the Capitol. Photo: L.U.C.E.
By courtesy of The Warburg Institute, University of London.

Preface

This book is about the relationship between Roman literature and one of its most obvious contexts, the city of Rome. Rome is a place, of course (one where at least some of the literature to be discussed here was written), but also an idea. Romans writing about Rome responded to the literary and historical associations of their city as much as to the city's material presence. Their responses in turn became part of the city, influencing the way later Romans – and others – thought of and wrote about Rome.

Rome's physical fabric has been appropriated and reappropriated over the centuries, by popes, princes, magistrates and Fascists. So too has the idea of Rome, a city endlessly rewritten, symbol at once of eternity and of the fragility of all human achievement, of the triumph of Christianity and of the lasting authority of the pagan republic of letters. For centuries, educated Europeans and Americans, immersed in classical literature, aspired to become, in a sense, Roman citizens, an aspiration which has left profound traces on much that has been written about the city itself. These later responses to Rome can, as I hope to demonstrate, offer suggestive insights into the written Romes of antiquity.

Rome as a place has been part of the inspiration for this project. My own experience of the city has been enriched by (and is inseparable from) encounters with a range of literary Romes written over 2,000 years. I am also happy to acknowledge the inspiration and assistance of friends and colleagues, from whom I have learnt a great deal in the course of writing this book. The series editors Denis Feeney and Stephen Hinds have been rigorous yet sympathetic readers of several versions. Charles Martindale and Duncan Kennedy have both read the manuscript in its entirety, subjecting it to their sometimes disconcertingly acute scrutiny. I have also benefited immensely from Nicholas Purcell's unmatched Roman erudition. Susanna Morton Braund, Wolfgang Ernst, Karen O'Brien, Ellen O'Gorman, Simon Price, Andrew Wallace-Hadrill and Thomas Wiedemann kindly read individual chapters and made me rethink some central issues. Seminar participants in Bristol, Oxford and Perugia asked challenging questions and offered perceptive comments. I am grateful to Paul Taylor for invaluable help with illustrations. Pauline Hire has been a splendid editor. Last but by no means least, I would like to thank Bernard Rafferty, whose support and encouragement made the final stages of writing this book a much more pleasurable experience.

This book was largely written while I was research fellow organising a project at the University of Bristol on Receptions of Rome in the nineteenth and twentieth centuries, funded by the Leverhulme Trust. Several visits to the British School at Rome proved very fruitful. The Arts Faculty Research Fund of the University of Bristol gave financial assistance.

Introduction: the city
of words

I could tell you how many steps make up the streets rising like stairways,
and the degree of the arcades' curves, and what kind of zinc scales cover
the roofs; but I already know that this would be the same as telling you
nothing. The city does not consist of this, but of relationships between the
measurements of its space and the events of its past ... As this wave of
memories flows in, the city soaks up like a sponge and expands.

(Italo Calvino *Invisible Cities*)

Rome is a city that has generated many books over the centuries – the
principal subject in countless travel memoirs, the evocative setting in a
host of poems and novels, and the object of a mass of scholarly literature.
Books have also played their part in generating Rome – or rather a
multiplicity of Romes. Modern visitors to the city wander among the
ruins of the Rome of Cicero – and also of the Romes of Petrarch, of
Gibbon, of Goethe, of Byron. Though particular visitors may not have
read the works of these authors, their writings (and many other literary
responses to the city) have profoundly conditioned the ways in which
Rome has been perceived.[1]

In antiquity, too, responses to Rome – that is to the physical fabric of
the city – were similarly conditioned. For the ancient inhabitant or
visitor, the buildings of Rome, the public spaces of the city, were crowded
with meanings and associations. These meanings were generated in part
through activities, political meetings, trials, religious rituals and so on,
associated with particular places. But Rome also took on meanings from

---

[1] Cf. Pemble (1987) 60–84; Varriano (1991); Buzard (1993). For a suggestive overview
of classical and post-classical responses to Rome, see Purcell (1992).

literature written about the city – stories of its foundation, praise of its splendid buildings, laments composed by those obliged to leave it. It is these literary resonances of the city and also the city's resonance in literature which will be the focus of my study.

An exploration of this complex territory necessarily draws on the approaches of different disciplines: in particular of history, archaeology and literary criticism. As regards the material city, recent decades have seen dramatic developments in knowledge of the topography of Rome, with a new focus on the functions of spaces and buildings from an historical perspective.[2] Filippo Coarelli, perhaps the most prominent figure in these developments, has strongly emphasised the need to refocus attention on combining the insights of archaeology with those of historical topography; this is a preoccupation shared by many classical archaeologists and ancient historians.[3] The strategies deployed by ancient literary texts in representing the city and its monuments have also received increasing attention from scholars in recent years. These investigations of Roman buildings and public spaces may be seen as exploring what might be termed, in Ann Vasaly's phrase, the city's 'metaphysical topography' – the symbolic associations of particular monuments and spaces within the context of the city as a whole.[4]

My aim in this book is to explore a few selected areas of the relationship between written Romes and material Romes. The first chapter examines the city of Rome as a repository for memories, personal but more particularly communal (here with particular reference to places associated with Romulus, Rome's founder). Virtually any city may be read as embodying its own past to some degree, but the ancient Romans had an especially strong sense of the relationship between places and memory. Two themes, adumbrated in Chapter 1, are brought out more explicitly in the following chapters. The material city's capacity to underwrite (or problematise) political power, whether of Rome over the rest of the empire or of particular rulers over the Roman world, is

---

[2] The significance of recent research with reference to the Forum Romanum is well emphasised by Purcell (1989). For a clear survey of recent work relating to Rome more generally, see Patterson (1992). This development is reflected in two recent works updating Platner and Ashby's magisterial volume of 1929: Richardson (1992) and the far more wide-ranging Steinby (1993–).

[3] Coarelli (1983), 6.

[4] Vasaly (1993), 41.

especially prominent in texts discussed in Chapters 3 and 4. Chapter 3 considers the changing symbolism of Rome's Capitoline hill, while Chapter 4 explores the associations, both positive and sinister, of Rome's great public buildings. My other major concern in this book is the relationship between the city of Rome and Roman identity. This issue receives particular attention in Chapters 2 and 5. Chapter 2 examines the city's religious identity and Rome's uneasy relationship with its mythical predecessor Troy. In the final chapter, the perspectives of Romans in exile will be compared with the perspectives of foreign visitors in later centuries, men and women so steeped in ancient literature that they feel themselves to be simultaneously aliens and Romans.

It is no accident that the Augustan era – a time when the material city was profoundly transformed – sees a new concern with the city in Roman texts. Some chapters of this book (particularly 1 and 2) are dominated by Augustan writers. Works of this period were to become points of reference for later Romans writing about the city and for authors many centuries later. I shall also consider Rome in republican texts – the city as it appears in the work of Varro and Cicero – and in works written under later emperors (by, in particular, the elder Pliny, the younger Seneca, Juvenal and Tacitus). Romans interpreted their city in a multiplicity of ways, as I shall try to emphasise. Through complex dialogues between texts and monuments were constructed the competing discourses which together have composed and continue to compose the city of Rome.

Imagining Rome

The resonant physical presence of Rome as a place we may personally experience can give us the sense that we are familiar with ancient Rome. When we think of the ancient city of Rome in its physical aspect, our perspective is almost inevitably dominated by the few structures which have survived in recognisable form. This Rome is liable to consist of such buildings as the Colosseum, the Pantheon, the baths. We too easily forget other structures – the temple of Capitoline Jupiter, the Saepta, the temple of the Sun – just as impressive in their time, which have now virtually disappeared. The Colosseum above all has come to stand for the Rome of pagan antiquity, in counterpoint to St Peter's, the emblem of Christian Rome. For ancient Romans – at least those who lived in or after the time of the Flavians – the Colosseum was also an important landmark, celebrated in the poems of Martial (*Spect.* 2). But it was one among many. If Romans had sought a single building to stand for their city, we may surmise they would have made a rather different choice – the temple of Capitoline Jupiter, perhaps.[5]

The modern visitor may feel there is a curious mismatch between the written city and the material city. Some of the most prominent material survivals from the ancient city have a low profile in ancient literary texts. The Pantheon, for instance, as rebuilt under Hadrian, though clearly a revolutionary structure in its own time, is scarcely mentioned.[6] This lack of fit between the literary and the material survivals is in part due to the simple fact that many of the texts describing Rome were written in the early principate, while most of the structures which have survived date from rather later. Nevertheless it has been a source of discomfort to generations of visitors to the city, who have arrived to discover ruins not of the city familiar to them from their reading – the broken walls of Cicero's house, perhaps, or the remains of Pompey's portico, where Caesar fell – but rather of a somewhat different, later city.[7] We must struggle then to imagine a city, or rather a succession of cities, in which different buildings dominated. Even for the most archaeologically erudite it is hard to imagine what these buildings looked like in their time. And it is perhaps even harder to imagine how Romans saw them.

Varronian Rome

Some of the most important buildings of antiquity have disappeared almost completely. The same is true of some of the books which most profoundly informed Roman perceptions of their city. Perhaps of greatest importance here are the treatises on the antiquities of Rome written in the late republic by Marcus Terentius Varro.[8] Varro, a man whose learning, according to the Christian writer Lactantius (*Inst.* 1.6.7),

---

[5] See Chapter 3, below.
[6] Though cf. Dio 53.27. On the revolutionary architecture of the Pantheon, see MacDonald (1976).
[7] Cf. Purcell (1992), 433–4. Fabricius' mid-sixteenth-century guidebook highlights this lack of fit. Cf. Tucker (1990), 83. McGowan (1994), 247–9 stresses the puzzlement of sixteenth-century French visitors.
[8] On the *Antiquitates*, see Dahlmann (1976) and Rawson (1985), esp. 233–48, 312–16. On the antiquarian tradition see Momigliano (1955), 67–106.

was unsurpassed among Romans and even Greeks, set out in his works to preserve Roman traditions, human and divine, from the oblivion which he felt threatened them. The *Antiquitates rerum humanarum* apparently consisted of twenty-five books, the *Antiquitates rerum divinarum* of sixteen (three of these were on sacred places).[9] As Augustine noted, Varro's interest was not in the human and divine generally but rather in the specifically Roman (*De civ. D.* 6.4).

Varro plainly conceived of the task he had undertaken in ambitious terms. Augustine writes:

cum vero deos eosdem ita coluerit colendosque censuerit ut in eo ipso opere litterarum suarum dicat se timere ne pereant, non incursu hostili, sed civium neglegentia, de qua illos velut ruina liberari a se dicit et in memoria bonorum per eius modi libros recondi atque servari utiliore cura quam Metellus de incendio sacra Vestalia et Aeneas de Troiano excidio penates liberasse praedicatur.

However, he [Varro] worshipped those same gods and judged their worship so important that he writes in that very work that he is afraid that they may disappear, not through some enemy attack, but through the carelessness of Rome's citizens. And he writes that through him they are freed from destruction and because of the nature of his books lodged in the memory of good men and preserved – an act of salvation more useful than that of Metellus, famous for rescuing the sacra of the temple of Vesta from the fire, or of Aeneas, celebrated for saving the Penates from the fall of Troy.

(Aug. *De civ. D.* 6.2 = 1, fr. 2a Cardauns)

Varro, in what is clearly a programmatic passage from the *Antiquitates rerum divinarum*, asserts a claim that the historian or antiquarian can do as much, if not more, to save Roman religion, to preserve Rome's past, as can a heroic leader such as Metellus or Aeneas. Varro, indeed, came to play a vital part in constituting the city of Rome as Romans (or at least educated Romans) perceived it. Much praised by Cicero (in a passage which will be examined below), the *Antiquitates* seem to have been a crucial source for many of the ancient writers who wrote about the city of Rome. A suggestive gauge of their importance, even in the fourth century CE, is the seriousness with which Varro's writings are treated in

[9] Augustine *De civ. D.* 6 is the most important source for the structure of Varro's work.

Augustine's *De civitate Dei*. Most of Book 6 is devoted to an attack on pagan religion, as it is set forth in Varro's work. Even at this late date, it seems, Varro had much to offer those who wanted to maintain their pagan Roman identity.[10]

Paradoxically it is Augustine, most articulate critic of Varro, whose work has perhaps done most to preserve Varro's *Antiquitates* (though it is not always clear how neatly Varronian passages can be separated from their Augustinian context). Even so, for us the *Antiquitates* have survived only in fragments, as disconnected and puzzling as the remains of the Roman forum – though we can gain some idea of the nature of Varro's writings about Rome from some sections of his *De lingua Latina* (in particular 5.144–65), a treatise on the Latin language which pays considerable attention to place names in the city. Even Rome's literary landscape then, apparently more durable than the material fabric of the ancient city, turns out to be fragmentary and full of gaps.

Writing the city

The material city was the creation of Roman magistrates, generals and emperors (or at least they took the credit for it). Writings about the city sometimes reflect their achievements. Yet we may also feel that the written cities to be found in the pages of Rome's antiquarians, historians and poets are sometimes in competition with the built cities of Rome's rulers. The opening of Livy's History suggests a strong parallel between the effort involved in the development of Rome and the task Livy himself has undertaken in recording that development: *res est praeterea et immensi operis, ut quae supra septingentesimum annum repetatur, et quae ab exiguis profecta initiis eo creverit ut iam magnitudine laboret sua*, 'Moreover, my subject involves immeasurable toil, for it must be traced back more than seven hundred years, and, starting from modest beginnings, it has so far grown that it is weighed down by its own immensity' (1.pr.4). *Res* here may be read both as the city of Rome and also as Livy's own work. Christina Kraus emphasises the parallel between 'the Urbs Livy is writing about and the *Urbs* he is writing'.[11] Numerous passages, particularly in the earlier books of his History, work to constitute the meanings associated with particular places in the city. Livy may be seen as, in Mary Jaeger's words, 'writing Rome into

---

[10] Cf. Momigliano (1963).   [11] Kraus (1994), 268.

existence, hill by hill'. The Manlius Capitolinus episode in Book 6, for instance, is read by Jaeger as an assertion of the superiority of literary history to the kind of history preserved by non-literary means such as monuments.[12] Livy presents himself as offering a version of the city better than the material constructions of Rome's rulers.

Horace, also writing in the time of Augustus, describes his own Odes as superior to built monuments: *Exegi monumentum aere perennius | regalique situ pyramidum altius*, 'I have built a monument more lasting than bronze and higher than the Pharaoh's pyramids' *(Carm.* 3.30.1–2). Jaeger has drawn attention to Horace's implied rivalry with Augustus in his role as rebuilder of the city. The treatment of the Campus Martius in a number of Horatian Odes, she argues, constructs a Campus consciously distinct from that created by the building work of Augustus and Agrippa. These and other literary texts may be seen as 'setting up a dialogue between the written and the material cities' which 'asserts the power of writing to record and define the city's meaning'[13] – though writing, in the form of inscriptions, was, of course, also an intrinsic part of many of the monuments of Augustan Rome. Another Augustan writer, Propertius, explicitly claims to be creating a city in his poems: *moenia namque pio coner disponere versu*, 'in loyal verse would I seek to set forth those walls' (4.1.57). The word *pius*, reminiscent of the Virgilian Aeneas, Augustus' alleged ancestor, can be read as implying deference to the princeps. Yet there is also a sense in which Propertius' written city is presented as of equal weight to that created by the emperor: *surgit opus* (4.1.67), referring to Propertius' own work, balances the rise of the material city charted in the opening lines of this programmatic poem.[14]

This trope was to have a long history. In the 1440s, at a time when the papacy was gradually re-establishing itself in Rome after decades of exile in Avignon, the humanist Flavio Biondo, a pontifical secretary, wrote a treatise *Roma instaurata*, 'Rome revived', dedicated to Pope Eugenius IV.[15] Biondo's work, informed by scholarship which was to remain

---

[12] Jaeger (1993).   [13] Jaeger (1990), 1, 139–75.
[14] Cf. Barchiesi (1994), 59. One might compare this with Propertius' allusion in 3.15 to the myth of Amphion, the lyre-player whose magical music had the power to create a city wall (as Duncan Kennedy has pointed out to me).
[15] The text is most readily accessible in D'Onofrio (1989). For discussion of this and other fifteenth-century texts on Roman antiquities see Greene (1982) and Spring (1972). I am grateful to Amanda Collins for drawing the latter to my attention.

unsurpassed for more than a century, draws extensively on ancient
literary texts to build up a picture of the physical form of the city in
antiquity. In his dedication, Biondo encourages the pope in his project of
restoring Rome's material fabric. But this project is conceived of as
complementary to, indeed dependent on, Biondo's own work – that of
reviving the ancient form of the city through a proper reading of ancient
texts.[16] Rome, through the ignorance of its inhabitants, has lost its
identity. *Ipse contendam, ut sic tu Romam per ingenioli mei literarum
monumenta, sicuti cementariorum fabrorumque lignariorum opera pergas
instaurare*, 'Let me insist, just as you strive to restore Rome, by means of
the work of many masons, architects and carpenters, so too you should
make use of the monuments set forth through the modest skill of my
writing' (pref.). His dedication concludes that posterity will judge: *utrum
. . . calce, latericio, materia, lapide aut aere, an literis facta solidior
diuturniorve maneat instauratio*, 'whether the restoration wrought in
marble, brick, cement, stone and bronze or the restoration in literature
will last better and longer'.

Later Rome

The following pages will consider not only the Romes of Livy, Virgil, and
other ancient writers but also the Romes of Petrarch, Gibbon and other
visitors and inhabitants of later centuries. For the Romes of these later
authors are infused with earlier versions of the city and they can often be
useful guides to hidden corners of written Rome, while even the best
known of ancient sites – and texts – can acquire new significance viewed
from this perspective.[17] It is also important to be aware of the many ways
in which these later 'receptions of Rome' have moulded our own
responses to the city. At the same time, we must recognise that our
responses – and theirs – are conditioned in part by present preoccupations,
which might include, in the late twentieth century, a concern with
cultural identity, or, in the late eighteenth, debates about rationality and
religious enthusiasm.

Edward Gibbon, in his autobiography, described his first visit to
Rome: 'At the distance of twenty-five years I can neither forget nor

---

[16] Cf. Spring (1972), 392, 403.
[17] On the benefits of 'reading backwards' see Martindale (1993).

express the strong emotions which agitated my mind as I first approached and entered the eternal city. After a sleepless night I trod with lofty step the ruins of the forum; each memorable spot where Romulus stood, or Tully spoke or Caesar fell was at once present to my eye.'[18] The quasi-religious nature of the sceptic Gibbon's language here is striking.[19] His vivid response to the material reality of Rome is not so much to the physical form of the places he sees but to their literary and historical associations.[20] Laurence Goldstein, in his discussion of John Dyer, quotes Horace Walpole's observation that Rome is a landscape where 'the memory sees more than the eyes'.[21] Another eighteenth-century visitor, Archibald Alison, wrote, 'And what is it that constitutes that emotion of sublime delight, which every man of common sensibility feels upon the first prospect of ROME? It is not the scene of destruction which is before him ... It is ancient Rome which fills his imagination. It is the country of Caesar, and Cicero, and Virgil which is before him.'[22] The physical city – in the late eighteenth century a mass of shapeless ruins and buildings from a bewildering variety of epochs – could make sense through, and also make sense of, ancient literary texts.[23] Rome derived its meaning from Romulus, Cicero and Caesar; at the same time these figures took on a new reality for Gibbon (and for other visitors) through Rome's physical presence.

But rather than digging at once down to the deepest level in Gibbon's reading, we might attempt a more nuanced literary stratigraphy. Gibbon was not only responding to ancient literary texts: he was also familiar with, for instance, Petrarch's letter to Giovanni Colonna, written after Petrarch had left Rome (*Rerum familiarum* 6.2), which describes the walks taken by the two of them around the city.[24] 'We used to wander together in that great city . . . and at each step there was present something which would excite our tongue and mind: here was the palace

[18] Gibbon (1897), 267. On the literary creation of Gibbon's visit to Rome see Craddock (1984).
[19] Cf. Jordan (1977), 7. As Charles Martindale has pointed out to me, Gibbon's language here could also be read as erotic.
[20] Similarly, at the end of the final chapter of *Decline and Fall* he speaks of 'visiting... the footsteps of heroes' (1909–14), VII 337.
[21] Goldstein (1977), 33.
[22] (1790), 28–9. I am grateful to Chloe Chard for this reference.
[23] Cf. Ernst (forthcoming) on Goethe's description of his own responses to Rome.
[24] Gibbon refers to this passage in Petrarch at (1909–14), VII 325 n.46.

of Evander, there the shrine of Carmentis, here the cave of Cacus, there the famous she-wolf and the fig-tree of Rumina with the more apt surname of Romulus . . . '[25] Petrarch goes on to list many other places in the city, proceeding not topographically but chronologically through Roman myth and history to the days of the Christian martyrs and finally Constantine.[26] Like Gibbon's Rome, Petrarch's city was filled with its past inhabitants, the figures he had come to know so well from his extensive study of classical literature. Petrarch's readings of Livy and Virgil in particular – whose Romes were known to him much earlier than was the physical city – thoroughly inform his responses to its material fabric. Gibbon too knew Rome first through books. He writes of Virgil's description of Rome in the time of Aeneas, 'This ancient picture so artfully introduced and so exquisitely finished must have been hugely interesting to an inhabitant of Rome; and our early studies allow us to sympathise in the feelings of a Roman.'[27] These writers, like many others, came to identify with the ancient Romans through their immersion in Latin literature, an experience which profoundly conditioned their responses to Rome itself.

Past and present

For Gibbon and for Petrarch, the past was almost unbearably present in Rome. Gibbon's first night in the city is sleepless, while Petrarch describes himself in what is presented as his first letter from Rome as (uncharacteristically) lost for words (*Rerum familiarum* 2.14).[28] Ancient authors, perhaps unwilling to admit to a time when Rome had ever been wholly unfamiliar to them, rarely respond so breathlessly to the city.[29] Yet this manner of viewing Rome – as a place where the past is irresistibly present – is in some ways foreshadowed in ancient literature about the city, literature in which these later visitors were so well read. Rome was

[25] Bernardo trans., p. 291
[26] For a discussion of the accuracy of Petrarch's archaeological and historical knowledge about Rome see Weiss (1969), 30–47.
[27] Gibbon (1909–14), VII 313 n. 3 on *Aeneid* 8.97–369.
[28] For similar responses on the part of renaissance French visitors, see McGowan (1994), 247.
[29] Though for silence as a response to the splendours of Rome cf. the discussion of Pliny in Ch. 4, below.

always already an especially time-laden space. Roman writers, with pride but also nostalgia, explored the tensions between Rome's modest origins and its later grandeur – tensions which they articulated in spatial terms. The Palatine, for instance, could be seen as at once Rome's most exclusive residential district and as the site of Romulus' primitive settlement (this trope, deployed particularly by Augustan writers, will be examined in detail in Chapters 1 and 2 below).

Ruins, indeed, had always been part of the city. The epigraph to this book comes from Varro's discussion of the Saturnian remains still visible on the Palatine. Even (or perhaps especially) Virgil's Aeneas, visiting the same hill, marked as the future site of Rome, sees ruins, traces of a lost past: *virum monimenta priorum*, 'monuments of earlier men' (8.312). These traces are a poignant reminder of the irrecoverability of the past, a sign of its profound absence. The age of Saturn, whose ruins still stand in Evander's proto-Rome, is a prelapsarian golden age which can never return. The use of ruins to evoke a superior past was to recur in many much later meditations on the site of the city.

Scenes of a city in ruins might also, even in antiquity, be read as foreshadowing Rome's own future. Philip Hardie has emphasised the implications for Rome of Lucan's portrayal of Julius Caesar at the ruins of Troy.[30] Lucan's description repeatedly echoes Virgil's account of Aeneas exploring the future site of Rome. Caesar *circumit exustae nomen memorabile Troiae*, 'wanders around Troy, famous only as the name of a city now destroyed' (9.964). Nature has continued the process of destruction begun by the Greeks:

> iam silvae steriles et putres robore trunci
> Assaraci pressere domos et templa deorum
> iam lassa radice tenent, ac nota teguntur
> Pergama dumetis: etiam periere ruinae.

> And now barren woods and rotting tree-trunks weigh down
> the house of Assaracus and clutch the temples of the gods in
> their worn roots; thorns cover renowned Pergama. Even the
> ruins have perished.   (9.966–9)

[30] Hardie (1992).

The same plants engulf the place that once was Troy in Lucan, *nota teguntur | Pergama dumetis*, and the place that will be Rome in Virgil, *silvestribus horrida dumis* (*Aen.* 8.348) – parallels between Rome and Troy in Lucan and other texts will be examined further in Chapter 2 below. This connection is reinforced by another echo of Virgil in the proem to Lucan's epic. Italy, the poet laments, lies in ruins as a result of the civil wars: *horrida . . . dumis multosque inarata per annos | Hesperia est desuntque manus poscentibus arvis*, 'Italy bristles with thorns, her land unploughed for years, and fields call out in vain for hands to till them' (1.28–9). As Hardie points out, Lucan's ruined Troy, foreshadowing a Rome in ruins once again, serves in particular to subvert the Virgilian vision of Rome as an empire without end.[31]

Rome may be called the 'eternal city' (a term whose history will be examined in Chapter 3), yet Rome has also been the city where the destructive workings of time have been most frequently lamented.[32] Those ancient texts which operate through a dialectic between Rome's rustic past and metropolitan present testify to the city's dramatic powers of transformation. The logic of such texts may be readily inverted to illustrate the equally dramatic transformation of the city from powerful capital to desolate ruin. For those who celebrated the rise of a new Christian empire from the ruins of pagan Rome, Rome's transformation could be a source of satisfaction. In the poems of Hildebert of Lavardin, Bishop of Tours, written in the twelfth century, the collapse of material pagan Rome, though described with classical echoes in elegiac terms, is ultimately a foil to the new Rome of St Peter – this time a truly eternal city.[33]

For erudite visitors of later centuries, however, the disappearance of the ancient Rome they knew so well from years of reading was rather to be viewed with ironic melancholy.[34] A guidebook to Rome published in the mid-sixteenth century by the German poet Georgius Fabricius quotes extensively from ancient and later texts (Horace, Virgil, Propertius, Ovid and others). These texts are presented as sources of information about the ancient city but also as a stimulus to the visitor's own emotional response.[35] Descriptions of the ruined state of the city in the sixteenth

---

[31] See too Martindale (1993), 49–51.
[32] Cf. Martindale (forthcoming).
[33] Krautheimer (1980), 200–2.
[34] On ruin literature see Janowitz (1990), 20–53; McGann (1984).
[35] Fabricius (1551). Cf. Tucker (1990), 58–9. On other guides of this period, also packed with quotations from ancient texts, see McGowan (1994), 250–5.

century are juxtaposed with passages from ancient authors, some describing directly the splendour of the city's appearance under Rome's emperors, others stressing the vast transformation Rome had undergone in turning from a small city-state to the capital of a vast empire. The complexity of time's legacy in Rome may only be understood through the ironies of such multiple juxtapositions.

The sixteenth-century French poet Joachim Du Bellay combines allusion to Virgil's description of the future site of Rome with elements of Lucan's picture of the ruins of Troy.[36] In his *Poemata* of 1558, Du Bellay writes:

> ille ego sum Thybris toto notissimus orbe,
>> quemque vides campum, maxima Roma fuit.
> nunc deserta iacet sylvestribus horrida dumis.

> I am that Tiber, known throughout the world. All of the
> plain you see was once mighty Rome. Now it lies deserted,
> overgrown with wild thorns.   (1.3.61–3)

Sylvestribus horrida dumis here echoes Virgil's Roman Capitol (*Aen.* 8.348), while the present nature of its desolation suggests also a scene of Lucanian ruin.[37] For later visitors to Rome, such as Du Bellay, the city's reversion to ruins was not a fear but a reality.[38]

The fall of Rome, mightiest of empires, was regularly interpreted as an example to later civilisations both of the vanity of human aspirations in general and also, specifically, of the dangers of imperial ambition. The English poet John Dyer in his 'The ruins of Rome', published in 1740, presents Rome as a negative model for the successor empire Britain. Here, as in many earlier laments for Rome's decayed state, we find a celebration of the aesthetic quality of ruins – even if this may be somewhat at odds with the moral of the poem.[39] Rome is made to serve Dyer's purposes through the medium of reverse Virgilian pastoral:

> And the rough reliquies of Carinae's street,
> Where now the shepherd to his nibbling sheep
> Sits piping with his oaten reed; as erst

---

[36] Cf. Tucker (1990), 61–2.
[37] As Tucker emphasises, there are also strong echoes of Propertius 4.1 here.
[38] On the reversion topos in general see Tucker (1990), 55–105.
[39] Goldstein (1977), 25–42; Janowitz (1990), 30–40.

> There piped the shepherd to his nibbling sheep,
> When the humble roof Anchises' son explored
> Of good Evander, wealth-despising king,
> Amid the thickets: so revolves the scene ...   (325–31)

Dyer here emphasises, as many had done before him, the parallel between the overgrown woodland of Rome in the time of the king Evander, described in *Aeneid* 8, and the site of the ancient city in his own time, reclaimed by rusticity.[40] The stress on Evander's virtuous frugality underlines Dyer's preoccupation with luxury as the force which eventually ruined Rome (echoing a concern widespread in ancient texts). Britons, for Dyer, must guard against a similar fate – though we might see a tension between his celebration of Evander's simplicity and his regret at Rome's (and potentially Britain's) return to such a state. Paradoxically then, despite Rome's profound transformation since antiquity, later writers have repeatedly made use of the Roman strategy of playing off past against present to articulate their own responses to the city in ruins.

Romantic ruin-poetry might refuse such historical dialogues. Byron's evocation of Rome in Canto IV of *Childe Harold* resists any attempt to plot a relationship between the city's textual survivals and its material remains. Instead he dwells on the impossibility of tracing Rome's history in its ruins:

> Chaos of ruins! who shall trace the void,
> O'er the dim fragments cast a lunar light,
> And say, 'here was, or is', where all is doubly night?   (IV 80)

For Byron, it is precisely this which makes being in Rome such a potent experience. What can survive of Rome is only: 'Tully's voice, and Virgil's Lay, | And Livy's pictur'd page' (82) – traces which cannot be neatly mapped onto the fragmentary remains of the city. Yet in the end Rome's very ruin is more resonant than these: 'Tully was not so eloquent as thou, | Thou nameless column with a ruined base' (110). The eloquence of Rome's ruins lies in their very unreadability. 'Whose arch or pillar meets me in the face, | Titus' or Trajan's? no – 'tis that of Time.' The aesthetic aspect of ruins here overwhelms their historical dimension.[41] In the end

---

[40] Among the best known earlier treatments of this is *De varietate fortunae* I of Poggio Bracciolini, who makes one of his characters quote Virgil's line, before continuing: *ut quidem is versus merito possit converti: 'Aurea quondam, nunc squalidis spinetis vepribusque referta'* 'So that line could with reason be changed: "Golden once, now overgrown with mean thistles and thorns"' (1993), lines 13–21. This motif was later appropriated by Gibbon in a passage to be discussed in Ch. 3, below.

all attempts at historical differentiation are futile: 'History . . . | Hath but one page' (108). As Anne Janowitz comments, this is an interiorised perspective on ruins, which comes close to total identification with them. Indeed Byron proclaims himself: 'a ruin amidst ruins' (25).[42]

Even for Byron, however, although the aesthetic aspect of Rome's ruins has routed the historical, although the dialogue between past and present has collapsed, yet in the end the significance of Rome's remains may be said to lie precisely in this broken relationship. Rome is a familiar world, profoundly defamiliarised. The pathos of Rome's ruins springs from the impossibility of matching up the tangible, present fragments of the material city with the intimately familiar, yet ultimately elusive, Rome known from literature. In the end, Byron's poem seems to move away in despair from Rome, from ruins, from the city which cannot ultimately escape time, to embrace the enormity of nature, in the form of the Ocean, 'the image of eternity' (183).

Despair as a response to Rome's ruins is suggestively dramatised in a watercolour painted a few decades earlier (1778–80) by the Swiss artist J. H. Fuseli, with the title 'The artist's despair before the grandeur of ancient ruins' (Plate 1). These ruins are recognisable as the giant hand and foot of a statue of Constantine, displayed in the courtyard of the Capitoline museum in Rome. Even for those who do not recognise the exact reference, however, these fragments are clearly marked as Roman (the letters 'SPQR' may be read on the base). The nature of the artist's despair remains open. Is it provoked by the impossibility of emulating the greatness of the past, still overwhelming even in ruins? By the knowledge that even the greatest works of art will decay? Or is it rather caused by the unassuageable longing for a closer contact with the long vanished dead? These ruins, though of vast stature, are yet human in form; the artist stretches out his hand to touch flesh that turns out to be cold, unresponsive stone.

Romans and aliens

The experience of visitors to Rome in later centuries, Gibbon's 'pilgrims from the remote and once savage countries of the north', might seem an unlikely parallel for the experience of Romans within their own city. But most of the writers whose texts will be concerning us here, Livy, Virgil,

[41] On Byron's lack of interest in the details known about Roman remains, see Springer (1987), 6–8.
[42] Janowitz (1990), 42–3.

Ovid, Propertius, Pliny, were born in provincial Italy. Rome would have been known to them first as a name and only later as a place. Indeed, we should not forget that literary texts were a first means of approach to the city for many in antiquity, just as they were for later visitors. A passage in Virgil's *Eclogues* is, however, unusual among ancient texts in its explicit evocation of a rustic perspective on the big city: *urbem quam dicunt Romam, Meliboee, putavi | stultus ego huic nostrae similem ... | verum haec tantum alias inter caput extulit urbes | quantum lenta solent inter viburna cupressi*, 'O Meliboeus, the city they call Rome I stupidly thought was like our own ... but that city holds its head above the others by as much as the cypresses stand above the supple osiers' (1.19–25).

The final chapter of this book will be particularly concerned with literature written at a distance from Rome. The sense of longing for lost Rome which often pervades the writings of exiles such as Cicero or Ovid in some ways parallels the longing to see Rome for the first time expressed by Petrarch, Goethe, Freud and many other later writers. Freud's desire for Rome was tinged with ambivalence. Leonard Barkan comments, 'he associates his failure to visit the city (at least before ... 1900) with the incompleteness of his own personal education and, more important, with the problematic of his entitlement to Roman, European or Christian culture. So it is that he identifies himself in his dreams with Hannibal, a Semite who never gained admittance to the eternal city.'[43] Barkan goes on to observe that the privilege of declaring *civis Romanus sum* was tantalisingly out of reach for many renaissance humanists also. In antiquity, too, one might add, *romanitas* could be an elusive quality.

Knowing Rome

Feeling at home in Rome was not a simple matter even for educated Romans of the late republic. Cicero, early in the *Academica*, pays a deferential compliment to the learned Varro:

> tum ego, 'sunt', inquam, 'ista, Varro; nam nos in nostra urbe peregrinantis errantisque tamquam hospites tui libri quasi domum reduxerunt, ut possemus aliquando qui et ubi essemus agnoscere ...'

> 'You are right, Varro,' I replied. 'For in our own city we were like foreigners wandering and drifting but your books brought us home, so that we might recognise who and where we were ...'   (1.9)

---

[43] Barkan (1991), 16–17.

The past ignorance on which Cicero comments is not an ignorance of the physical aspect of the city, intimately familiar to himself and his companions who had lived and worked there almost all their lives. Rather to know Rome, to possess Rome as one's true home, one must know what Rome means. Varro's books, as Cicero goes on to say, documented 'the age of Rome, the chronology of its history, the laws of its religion and priesthood, its civil and military institutions, the topography of its districts and places, and the terminology, classification and moral and rational basis of all the Romans' religious and secular institutions' (leaving aside his insights into literature, language and philosophy). In Cicero's account, this system of erudition plays the part of a metaphysical street map of the city.

The antiquarian's knowledge is what has made Rome a familiar place – and also given Varro's readers a firmer sense of their own identity. Cicero's simile suggestively conveys what a learned Roman might mean by 'a sense of place'. It also sets up an intriguing version of the distinction between Romans and non-Romans. To be at home in Rome was not to be born there (how many Romans could make that boast?). It was rather to be master of Roman knowledge. Without such knowledge, Romans might be thought to imperil their own identity, while, by implication, Roman knowledge could confer *romanitas* on the foreigner.

Knowledge of Rome's past was essential for those seeking to find their way in the city. At the same time, the city itself played a part in mediating relationships between present and past Romans. Particular places in the city, especially public places, might serve as a stimulus to memories of particular events and individuals from earlier times. In Cicero's *De finibus* the character Piso is made to comment:

> equidem etiam curiam nostram (Hostiliam dico, non hanc novam, quae minor esse videtur posteaquam est maior) solebam intuens Scipionem, Catonem, Laelium, nostrum vero in primis avum cogitare.

> Even when I saw our senate house (the Curia Hostilia I mean, not the new one, which seems to me lesser since it has become greater in size), Scipio, Cato, Laelius and above all my own grandfather would come before my mind.[44]   (*Fin.* 5.2)

---

[44] Sulla had enlarged the old curia a few years before the dramatic date of the dialogue. See Van Deman (1922).

The city was a storehouse of Roman memories, an archive which ordered them and made them accessible.

For Romans, places were especially resonant as reminders of past events and individuals. In Cicero's *De legibus* Atticus is made to observe *movemur enim nescio quo pacto locis ipsis, in quibus eorum, quos diligimus aut admiramur, adsunt vestigia*, 'for we are moved in some mysterious way by places which bear the traces of those whom we love and admire' (2.4).[45] Cicero goes on in the next chapter to comment on his feelings for Arpinum, the small town where he was born. At the same time Cicero remarks, though in less detail, on his even stronger attachment to Rome, for every Roman has two *patriae*. Vasaly has elegantly drawn out the implications of this collocation: 'The description ... of Cicero's emotional attachment to places that spoke to him of his own history and identity reflects the deeper connections of Romans to places in Rome of communal symbolic significance.'[46]

Livy's History repeatedly stresses attachment to place as a powerful motive force in the development of Rome. Romulus and Remus, in his narrative, founded Rome on this particular site partly out of sentimental attachment to the place where they had been exposed and brought up (1.6.3). At the opening of Book 2, love of place is invoked as a vital bond, holding the community together. It would have been dangerous to have given liberty to the motley inhabitants of Rome before such time as their aspirations had been united by *pignora coniugum ac liberorum, caritas ipsius soli, cui longo tempore adsuescitur*, 'the pledges of wives and children and love of the place itself, a feeling which takes much time to develop' (2.1.5). Livy's most extended discussion of the Roman feeling for the physical site of the city comes at a turning-point in his narrative, the end of Book 5, when Camillus persuades the Romans not to abandon their city (5.54.3) – a passage which will be discussed at length in Chapter 2, below. For many of Livy's readers, of course, Rome was not a place made dear through long familiarity. Madeleine Bonjour reads Livy's insistence on the love Rome inspires as an attempt to translate affection for one's native place (whether Padua, Arpinum, Sulmo or any other relatively small community) into an affection for the great city to which so many of its citizens were attached by law rather than by birth.

---

[45] For a similar sentiment see Sen. *Ep.* 49.1.
[46] Vasaly (1993), 33. NB also Bonjour (1975b), 165–7 and (1975a), esp. 1–162.

First city?

Part of Rome's meaning is and was inevitably constituted in its difference from other places. An important axis of difference in antiquity was that between city and countryside. Young Romans were regularly set the task of debating the relative merits of city and country (a practice whose literary resonances will be discussed in Chapter 5). The part of the city in such debates is, even if only implicitly, always played by Rome. Though Rome itself might be represented as having once been rural, as we saw above, yet Rome in the present, for writers of the late republic and principate, is irretrievably urban (only the richest could afford the piquant luxury of re-creating rustic simplicity in the heart of the city).[47] Rome is often referred to in Latin literature simply by the term *urbs*.

Even when other cities were acknowledged, Rome itself remained pre-eminent. Yet there is also a sense in which the particular resonance of Rome is negotiated against that of other cities. The relationship between Rome and Troy will be discussed in Chapter 2. Troy was pre-eminently the city of the past. Even within the Roman empire, other large cities flourished in the present, Antioch and Alexandria the largest among them. These great cities must have had some features in common with the empire's capital (though they are much less well documented than Rome itself). Alexandria had been celebrated in the time of the Ptolemies as capital of the world.[48] The seat of the Egyptian rulers, who had (allegedly) set their sights on control of the Roman empire but were finally defeated by Augustus, was viewed with continuing disquiet long after Egypt became part of Roman territory.[49] Alexandria is regularly mentioned in connection with the plans of Roman leaders (Mark Antony, Julius Caesar, Caligula, Nero) seeking an alternative capital to Rome. Alexandria as potential capital continues to symbolise the possibility of an eastern, decadent, tyrannical regime, thus reinforcing the association of the city of Rome with tradition and moderate rule.

The cities of the Greek world, such as Pergamon, Corinth, Halicarnassus, had provided an aesthetic challenge to Rome in earlier centuries; in the third and second centuries BCE, particularly, Roman leaders competed

---

[47] On subversions of city/country distinctions as a form of luxury see Purcell (1987) and Edwards (1993), 148–9.
[48] Ceausescu (1976), 98.
[49] Ceausescu (1976).

to secure the services of the most fashionable Hellenistic architects for their victory monuments – though it was only under Augustus that Rome acquired an overall physical appearance which was felt to be commensurate with the city's world-dominating position.[50] Greek cities challenged Rome not only in terms of their glamorous physical appearance but also through their massive and long-standing cultural prestige. A number of Roman texts may be read as consciously or unconsciously stressing the ways Rome differed from (and was superior to) the cities of the Greek world. Cicero in *De republica* contrasts the location of Rome with that of most Greek cities – Rome is ideally situated on a river, somewhat inland, thereby avoiding the corrupting influences of a location directly on the sea (2.5–8).[51] The downfall of the great city of Corinth (and cities like it) Cicero attributes to the fact that its citizens were, because of their maritime situation, tempted away from warfare and agriculture to commerce. Thus Rome, through its inland location, managed to retain its moral superiority. When, in Thucydides' History, Pericles praises Athens, he is made to point to the city's powerful trading position (2.38) – all the good things of the world come to Athens; Athenians enjoy the use of foreign imports as easily as local produce. Indeed the literary traditions of praise of Greek cities often concentrated on their positions as powerful entrepôts. Praise of Rome and Italy, however, tended to focus on Italian self-sufficiency – the wide range of produce from fertile Italy making imports unnecessary.[52] By the late republic, Rome was surely more a centre for cosmopolitan consumption than a model of traditional Italian frugality. This rhetorical tension gives some hint of the degree to which discussions of Rome might be conditioned by a concern to differentiate the city from other cities.

Urban politics

The city of Rome has an important role to play in Ciceronian oratory. The eloquence of Cicero made the stones speak – for example, in defence of Scaurus, with whose ancestors' services to the city Cicero connected the most evocative buildings on view to his listeners (*Scaur.* 46–8), and

[50] Gros (1976b).
[51] A number of Cicero's arguments are adapted from Plato *Laws* 704d-e.
[52] Cf. Labate (1984), 51–64. Though writers such as the elder Pliny also celebrate the wealth of goods available in Rome as an index of Roman power (see Ch. 4 below).

against Catiline, indicted by Rome's sacred places (*Cat.* 4.18).[53] Quintilian, in his treatise on the education of an orator (5.10.41), comments on the role of arguments connected with places in arousing praise and blame. Such appeals to the visible environment are almost unknown in Greek oratory.[54]

Cicero's enlistment of buildings in pleading legal cases in some ways parallels the more concrete role of the city and its buildings in other struggles between leading Romans. Recent scholarship has effectively charted the importance of building to elite self-presentation in the late republic.[55] Prominent generals erected splendid temples paid for from the spoils of their great campaigns along the course of the route taken by the triumphal procession – a striking example of the way in which ritual served to articulate the topography of Rome.[56] Such temples, usually equipped with inscriptions advertising their builders' names and accomplishments, reminded citizens of a general's great service to the city. In later years, his descendants might continue to take responsibility for maintenance and restoration, thus parading their connection with these visible reminders of their ancestors' achievements.

With autocracy the role of the city changed. No longer an arena for aristocratic competition in building, it became the most powerful medium for displays of the imperial image.[57] The city of brick became a city of marble. Emperors appropriated the past in physical ways, Augustus first and perhaps most strikingly. Paul Zanker has set out, for instance, the means by which the Forum Romanum became a monument to the Julio-Claudians.[58] Later emperors, especially Caligula, Nero and Hadrian, strove to appropriate the monuments of their predecessors – or else to outdo them.[59]

---

[53] Cicero advises the would-be orator to make use of his surroundings *De or.* 2.266–7 (discussed by Millar (1986); Vasaly (1993), 34–5).

[54] As Vasaly has emphasised (1993), 26. Hence, she adds, the fact that such appeals are not well accommodated into ancient schemes of rhetorical theory (largely developed by Greek rhetoricians).

[55] See e.g. Eck (1984).

[56] Gros (1976b). A clear account is given of the main developments in Stambaugh (1988), Chs.2 and 3. On the triumphal route see Coarelli (1968). For the inter-relationship between ritual and landscape in Rome see Cancik (1985).

[57] Zanker (1988).

[58] Zanker (1988), 79–82.

[59] On Nero's building, see Elsner (1994). On that of Hadrian see Boatwright (1987).

This strategy may have been so tremendously effective precisely because the Roman sense of history was so heavily invested in places. Romans of the late republic remembered the story of the patrician–plebeian struggle (the narrative which dominates Livian early republican history) in topographical terms. The Aventine hill was perpetually associated with the secession of the plebs.[60] The temple of Concord, allegedly built by Camillus in 367 BCE on the lower slopes of the patrician Capitoline, marked the conclusion of this struggle. The temple was later appropriated for conservative ends by L. Opimius, who rebuilt it in 121 BCE to celebrate the senate's victory over Gaius Gracchus.[61] In 1347, Cola di Rienzo called a meeting on the Aventine to plan a popular revolt against aristocratic domination – a gesture which suggests a sophisticated understanding of the importance of place in Roman political history.[62]

Nicholas Purcell comments on the extent to which ancient Romans relied on monuments as evidence for the earliest days of Rome's history: 'the most eloquent texts about the origins of the city available to the Romans of the middle and late republic were the terracotta-clad buildings themselves, their inter-relationships and the rites which articulated them'.[63] Peter Wiseman has also emphasised the importance of monuments to Roman historians as sources for narratives. Monuments were often misinterpreted, he argues, or used as 'evidence' for imaginative reconstructions of the past, but they might also serve as corroboration for more accurate accounts of past events. Remains have been found of a monument celebrating the achievements in 264 BCE of M. Fulvius Flaccus, which seems to have been destroyed in the late third century BCE. Wiseman links the destruction of this monument with the development of a different account of the events of 264 preserved in the narrative of *De viris illustribus* which gives to Decius Mus and Appius Caudex credit for Fulvius' achievements, commenting 'the destruction of the *monumentum* itself must have made it much easier for the false version to gain currency'.[64] To efface a monument was to efface part of Rome's history –

---

[60] Livy 2.28.1; 3.50–54; 3.67. This association was appropriated by Gaius Gracchus (Plut. *C. Gracch.* 16.4–5; Appian *BC* 1.26).

[61] For the details see Steinby (1993–), *s.v.*, though the association with Camillus is called into question by Momigliano (1941).

[62] *The Life of Cola di Rienzo* 1.4.

[63] Purcell (1989), 165.

[64] Wiseman (1986).

though, as Livy emphasises, literature might work to preserve the memory of vanished monuments.[65]

Roman history might also be rewritten through new buildings. The ranks of statues flanking the temple of Mars Ultor in Augustus' new Forum Augustum, the Julii on one side, other Roman heroes on the other, can be seen as monumentalising a detailed yet sweeping claim concerning the importance of one particular family, that of Augustus' forebears, the Julii, in Roman history.[66]

Seducing Rome

Scholars of Rome's built environment have tended to concentrate on reconstructing the impact of new buildings as it may have been intended by the builder. Paul Zanker's work, for instance, offers many persuasive readings of Augustan monuments, teasing out the ideological nuances of their iconographic programmes. The experience of walking through a part of the Augustan city is suggestively reconstructed by Diane Favro, whose study of the Campus Martius highlights the ways in which Augustus' interventions in the urban fabric may be seen as constructing an 'engrossing urban narrative' out of what had been an indecipherable jumble.[67] But some Romans at least may have resisted such a narrative – whether because they lacked the historical and mythical knowledge needed to make the connections, or because they chose to interpret Rome's new monuments within different paradigms.

Builders could not altogether control the ways in which their new constructions were read. Catullus (in poem 55) presents himself as looking for a friend in the Portico of Pompey's theatre complex (built with the proceeds of his great eastern campaigns), which seems in Catullus' poem to be a place notoriously full of sexually available women – not perhaps inappropriate in a monument dominated by a shrine to Venus but not necessarily how the great general would have liked his works to be thought of.[68] Propertius too, in his Elegies,

---

[65] Cf. Jaeger (1993).
[66] The iconology of the Forum is set out in Zanker (1968). See also Zanker (1988), esp. 210–15. For an exploration of the relationship between the *elogia* of the statues in the forum and the versions of the stories in Livy's History see Luce (1990).
[67] Zanker (1988); Favro (1993).
[68] Jaeger (1990), 23–30. Pompey's portico has similar associations in Propertius 2.32.11 and 4.8.75.

sometimes makes use of Rome's most recent adornments as a backdrop to his love affairs.

And Ovid, writing under an older, less forgiving Augustus, also appropriates the monuments of imperial Rome for erotic purposes. Indeed, Ovid is much more thorough-going in his deployment of the city of Rome as the natural environment for the activities which form the subject of love poetry.[69] The colonnade of the Danaids, adjoining the Temple of Apollo on the Palatine (one of the most high-profile monuments of the Augustan building programme), features in *Amores* 2.2.3–4 as a good place to meet attractive girls. The portico plays a similar role in its three appearances in the *Ars amatoria*.[70] Other Augustan monuments too are taken over for romantic assignations: the Porticus Liviae and Porticus Octaviae (*Ars am.* 1.71–2; 3.391). Ovid's reference to the temple of Jupiter (whose precinct was restored by Augustus in the 20s BCE) in *Tristia* 2 is especially suggestive:

> quis locus est templis augustior? haec quoque vitet,
>   in culpam siqua est ingeniosa suam,
> cum steterit Iovis aede, Iovis succurret in aede
>   quam multas matres fecerit ille deus.

> What place could be more august than the temples? These too
> should be avoided by any woman whose nature inclines her to
> wrong. As she stands in Jupiter's temple, it will occur to her in
> Jupiter's temple how many women that god has made mothers.
>   (2.287–90)

The pun on Augustus' name (*augustior*) emphasises the emperor's personal connection with so many of the temples in Rome (religion played a major part in Augustus' presentation of himself as restorer of past Roman values). Augustus' relationship to Jupiter gives this passage a particular significance. Ovid, like many other poets, compared Augustus' position on earth to that of Jupiter in heaven (*Fasti* 2.131–2). But if Jupiter models for Augustus, what might it mean to say that he has caused many women to be mothers? Augustus' marriage legislation (the *lex Iulia de maritandis ordinibus* of 18 BCE, later modified by the *lex Papia Poppaea* of 9 CE) ostensibly aimed at inducing women to have children.

---

[69] Cf. Labate (1984), 58.
[70] *Ars am.* 1.73–4; 1.492; 3.389. See Rudd (1976), 13–14.

But Augustus' responsibility for their maternity was to be rather more indirect than that of Jupiter in the myths Ovid alludes to; the comparison makes a strange compliment to the moral emperor.

Tristia 2 seeks to persuade its addressee that works of literature and art, rituals and monuments, rarely succeed in having only the consequences their creators intended, in being used only in the ways they foresaw. The readings of a poem (the author of the *Ars amatoria* argues in self-defence) cannot be controlled by the author; the interpretations of a monument cannot be controlled by the builder. Thus Ovid artfully 'misreads' the Augustan city; the sober monuments of *Roma*, celebrations of great victories on the battlefield, were always liable to be inverted and appropriated for Rome's mirror image and secret name, *amor* – or for other purposes.

Fragments

Our perceptions of the city are conditioned not only by verbal texts but also by images. Two of the four illustrations I have chosen for this book are pictures of Rome engraved in the mid eighteenth century by Giovanni Battista Piranesi, whose work has deeply influenced the responses to Rome of generations of visitors. Piranesi, in his Scenographia of the Campus Martius (Plate 2), deploys his daunting imaginative powers to summon up a Rome of ruins in a desert – we can make out the Pantheon, Domitian's stadium (now beneath the Piazza Navona), Augustus' mausoleum and a handful of other monuments. In the foreground of the picture, dwarfing these standing ruins, are heaped up assorted fragments of Rome's past greatness: among them broken inscriptions bearing the names of the emperors Augustus and Claudius, part of a gigantic architrave (celebrating Piranesi's friend Robert Adam), and some obelisks, translated to the Campus Martius from Egypt.[71] Profoundly defamiliarised, this is a Rome which can exist only in the imagination – for the Campus Martius, at least, has been continuously inhabited since antiquity. The image serves paradoxically to suggest the impossibility of stripping Rome down to its ancient skeleton. The fragments of the ancient city are inextricably embedded in the structures of later centuries and can only be laid bare by annihilating the Rome of the present, as

---

[71] On this image see Wilton-Ely (1978), 74.

Piranesi's phrase in the title of the picture *e ruderibus nostri* ... *aevi aedificiis*, 'from the ruins of the buildings of our own age', implies.

The maps and models of ancient Rome most widely in circulation today, useful though they are, generally present us with a sanitised, depopulated image of Rome in the fourth century CE. The present book contains no map of Rome. Any such map would inevitably present a frozen snapshot of the city at a particular moment, whether the late fourth century or the death of Augustus. For orientation I have included only another picture by Piranesi, his masterplan of the city (from *Antichità Romane*), an image of the underlying topography of the city's hills and valleys, surrounded by fragments of the Severan marble plan known as the Forma Urbis (Plate 3).[72] Piranesi's image presents the viewer with an impossible puzzle. Although they represent the same city in space, the fragments cannot be mapped onto the plan for they represent different cities in time. While the plan shows the outline of the Baths of Diocletian, there will of course be no sign of this vast structure on the Forma Urbis, produced decades before the baths were built. Thus Piranesi's fragmentary map of Rome highlights, rather than effaces, Rome's extraordinary chronological complexity.

[72] Wilton-Ely (1978), 48–51.

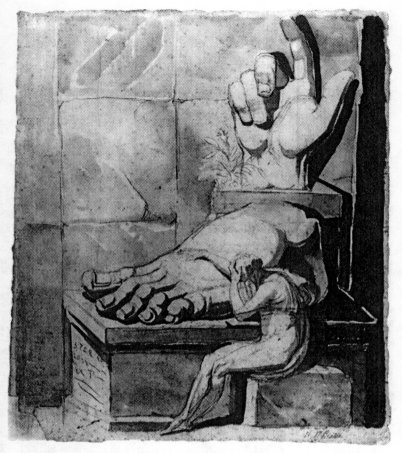

Plate 1. 'The artist's despair before the grandeur of ancient ruins',
Henry Fuseli, c. 1778/80. Kunsthaus Zurich, Zurich (Switzerland).

Plate 2. 'Scenographia' from *Il Campo Marzio dell' Antica Roma*, G. B. Piranesi, 1762

Plate 3. Plan of Rome from *Antichità Romane de' Tempi della Repubblica e de' Primi Imperatori,*
G. B. Piranesi, 1748.

Plate 4. Mussolini addressing young Fascists on the Capitol.

CHAPTER

I

The city of memories

Freud, in his essay 'Civilisation and its Discontents' (published in 1930), takes as an analogy for the human mind the city of Rome. Like Piranesi's engraving, this text highlights Rome's chronological complexity:

Let us, by a flight of the imagination, suppose that Rome is not a human habitation but a psychical entity with a similarly long and copious past – an entity, that is to say, in which nothing that has come into existence will have passed away and all the earlier phases of development exist alongside the later ones. This would mean that in Rome the palaces of the Caesars and the Septizonium of Septimius Severus would still be rising to their old height on the Palatine and the castle of S. Angelo would still be carrying on its battlements the beautiful statues which graced it until the siege by the Goths and so on. But more than this. In the place occupied by the Palazzo Cafarelli would once more stand – without the Palazzo having to be removed – the Temple of Juppiter Capitolinus; and this not only in its latest shape, as the Romans of the empire saw it, but also in its earliest one, when it still showed the Etruscan forms and was ornamented with terracotta antefixes. Where the Coliseum now stands we could at the same time admire Nero's vanished Golden House. On the piazza of the Pantheon we should find not only the Pantheon of today, as it was bequeathed to us by Hadrian, but, on the same site, the original edifice erected by Agrippa; indeed, the same piece of ground would be supporting the church of Santa Maria sopra Minerva and the ancient temple over which it was built. And the observer would perhaps only have to change the direction of his glance or his position in order to call up the one view or the other.[1]

[1] Freud (1985), 257–8.

Rome becomes a palimpsestic city, which may be read from different directions at different levels to tell every episode in the city's history.[2] This kaleidoscopic vision is a work of both imagination and erudition. It requires a viewer steeped in Rome's history, sensitive to the nuance and association of Etruscan terracotta, Neronian gold, Gothic barbarism and militant Christianity. Despite his feelings of ambivalence towards the Christian, western culture which Rome had come to represent, Freud here displays his own mastery of Roman history, his participation in one of the forms of knowledge which had traditionally marked membership of European elites.

Freud sets up an image of place as time made visible. As Bakhtin comments in setting out his notion of the chronotope, narratives must always represent space in the dimension of time: 'Time, as it were, thickens, takes on flesh, becomes artistically visible; likewise, space becomes charged and responsive to the movements of time, plot and history.'[3] Different forms of narrative operate with very different chronotopes. In Freud's vision a particular notion of time–space relationship is called into play which seems to erode historical differenti-ation.[4] In Barkan's words, Freud's description presents Rome in a 'synchronous, permanent present'.[5]

This strategy is suggestively close, I want to argue, to the ways many ancient writers responded to their city's past. Roman writers regularly use space to explore the relationship between past and present. Such treatments of place implicitly offer a direct mode of access to moments from the past, an access not mediated through the complex structure of historical narrative (though often, as with Freud's description of Rome, a detailed knowledge of the associations of different episodes in Roman history on the part of the reader or listener is assumed). Places may be made to affirm Roman continuities in such texts (as in the case of Cicero's reference to the curia, below), yet the juxtaposition of vastly different images of the past and present states of particular locations in the city often serves to emphasise Rome's lack of continuity, the tension between

---

[2] As Ernst points out (forthcoming), Freud based his description on the seamless narrative of early Rome in the first edition of *CAH* VII. The fragmentary city which emerges or rather fails to emerge from scholarly accounts transmitted in the new edition of *CAH* VII would not so easily lend itself to such treatment.

[3] Bakhtin (1981), 84.

[4] Cf. Janowitz (1990), 51.

[5] Barkan (1991), 13.

past rusticity and present urbanity, and thus to problematise what it means to be a Roman.

For Romans, places were especially significant as repositories for memory, both personal and national.[6] In the fifth book of Cicero's *De finibus* the narrator describes a conversation between Cicero and some friends on a visit to Athens. One character, Piso, is made to respond as follows on visiting Plato's Academy:

> tum Piso: 'naturane nobis hoc', inquit, 'datum an errore quodam, ut, cum ea loca videamus in quibus memoria dignos viros acceperimus multum esse versatos, magis moveamur quam si quando eorum ipsorum aut facta audiamus aut scriptum aliquod legamus? velut ego nunc moveor. venit enim mihi Platonis in mentem, quem accepimus primum hic disputare solitum ...'

> Then Piso said: 'Are we prompted, I wonder, by nature or by fantasy when, on seeing places which we know to have been the favourite haunts of distinguished men, we are more moved than when we hear of their deeds or read something that they have written? Such is the emotion I now feel. For Plato comes before my mind – tradition says it was here he used to debate ...'   (Cic. *Fin.* 5.2)

The stress on emotion is clear in this and other passages in Cicero describing responses to place, as Vasaly has recently emphasised.[7] Piso goes on to describe the emotional associations of several other places (in Rome as well as Greece) before concluding: ... *tanta vis admonitionis in locis; ut non sine causa ex iis memoriae ducta sint disciplina*, 'Places have so great a power of suggestion that the technical art of memory is with good reason based upon them.'

The art of memory is not discussed further in the *De finibus*, but in the *De oratore* Cicero describes in some detail this technique for memorising the topics to be covered in a speech.[8] The orator is advised to imagine a space, such as a basilica, with individual niches and corners. The topics to be remembered are then associated, in the order in which they are to be recalled, with these spaces. As he speaks, the orator is to imagine himself walking around the building and what he sees will remind him of the

---

[6] Cf. Vasaly (1993), intro.

[7] Vasaly (1993), 29–33.

[8] *De or.* 2.351–4. Cf. *Ad Herenn.* 3.29–40 and Quint. *Inst.* 11.2.17–22. These texts are discussed by Yates (1966), 1–26; Vasaly (1993), 100–2.

topics he is to mention. The order is fixed by the sequence of places in the building. In this mnemonic exercise, space is used to organise memory. For these purposes, the space itself need not have its own associations. Yet it is clear from the words Cicero gives to Piso that Romans might see a connection between this use of space to organise memory and a much more emotive association between particular spaces and particular memories. Indeed Piso is made to imply that it was the particular power of the associations of space for Romans which made the art of memory based on *loci* so effective.

Cicero's Piso compares the effect of visiting the Academy with that of reading Plato's works and claims that places have more power to move us than texts. For some purposes, places might play the part of texts. One of the interlocutors in Cicero's treatise *De legibus* is made to observe that, in contrast to the other literary forms flourishing in Cicero's day, *dest . . . historia litteris nostris*, 'history is lacking in our national literature' (1.5). In the republic, at least, the city itself was Rome's chief historical text. Topography functioned as a substitute for literary narrative. Florence Dupont suggests:

> Roman memory, lacking any anchorage in the inspired works of ancient poets, was rooted in the sacred ground of the city. To walk around Rome was to travel through its memory, past Romulus' cabin, Cacus' rock and Egeria's wood.[9]

This comment perhaps disregards a number of writers such as Ennius, whose *Annales* was certainly concerned with Rome's history, but Dupont is surely right to emphasise the historical resonance of Roman topography.[10]

Under the principate, historical narratives of Rome's past were not so scarce. Yet literary accounts, in particular Livy's History and Virgil's *Aeneid*, themselves celebrated the mythological and historical associations of particular places in the city of Rome. And as these works acquired a central role in the educational curriculum, responses to the 'sacred ground' of the city would in turn have been informed by Virgilian and Livian views of Roman history.

In this chapter, I shall explore this Roman sense of space by taking up

[9] Dupont (1992), 74.
[10] Cf. Purcell who observes that for later Romans, the city was the only available text for early Roman history (1989), at 165.

one of the examples cited by Dupont, the cabin or hut of Romulus – known as the *casa* or *tugurium Romuli* – examining both the hut itself and also the literary and political ends to which it was deployed. As a preliminary we might look again at Virgil's palimpsestic view of the city (which does not explicitly mention the hut of Romulus). In Book 8 of the *Aeneid*, Aeneas visits what will in later centuries become the site of Rome (a passage often used by later writers to articulate their own responses to Rome, as we saw earlier). The Arcadian Evander, already settled there, takes Aeneas on a tour of the site, culminating on the Capitol:

> hinc ad Tarpeiam sedem et Capitolia ducit,
> aurea nunc, olim silvestribus horrida dumis.

> Hence to the Tarpeian citadel he leads him and the Capitol,
> golden now, then rough with woodland thickets. (*Aen.* 8.347–8)

Here a multi-layered sense of place is conveyed in part by the use of names – *Tarpeiam* and *Capitolia* - which the area would not receive until later (the legend of Tarpeia was associated with the time of Aeneas' descendant, Romulus; etymologisers associated the term 'Capitol' with the discovery of a buried human head during the construction, under Tarquinius, of the temple of Jupiter Optimus Maximus). Also notable is the contrast between the sylvan aspect of the place in Evander's time and the golden Capitol of the future (in particular the time of Augustus) – though, as James Zetzel has noted, the word *olim* may also look forward to a time still further in the future when the Capitol will once again be overgrown.[11] Thus it would come to resemble once again the overgrown ruins of monuments built by Janus and Saturn, which Evander points out to his visitor a few lines later (355–8) – Rome's ruined past is part of the city even before its foundation, as we saw in the Introduction, above. I shall return below to the moral associations of the contrasting pictures of pastoral and Augustan Rome. The contrast itself is echoed in Virgil's representation of another hill, the Palatine, where the tour ends at Evander's humble hut:

[11] Jackson Knight Memorial Lecture, delivered at University of Exeter, 6 May 1993. The double vision of Rome conveyed here is also discussed by Wiseman (1984). For a parallel chronological doubleness in Virgil see *Aeneid* 6.773–6, discussed by Feeney (1986), esp. 7–8. Evocations of pastoral Rome will be discussed further in Ch. 2, below.

talibus inter se dictis ad tecta subibant
pauperis Evandri, passimque armenta videbant
Romanoque foro et lautis mugire Carinis.
ut ventum ad sedes, 'haec' inquit 'limina victor
Alcides subiit, haec illum regia cepit.
aude, hospes, contemnere opes et te quoque dignum
finge deo, rebusque veni non asper egenis.'

As they spoke, they drew near the home of Evander – the
house of a poor man – and on all sides they saw cattle lowing
in the Roman forum and in smart Carinae. When they had
come to the house, Evander said: 'Victorious Hercules
himself stooped to cross my threshold. This palace welcomed
him. Have the courage, guest, to look down on wealth and
make yourself too worthy of divinity. Enter with charity
towards my humble estate.'   (*Aen.* 8.359–65)

Cattle low in the area which will become the Roman forum. We are
discreetly reminded, by the mention of another fashionable address,
lautis ... Carinis – 'smart Carinae' – that the Palatine was to become the
most desirable residential area in Rome in later centuries.

When Virgil was writing, this was the part of Rome where the emperor
Augustus lived. But for Romans of that time it would not have been
necessary to read the *Aeneid* to be made aware of a contrast between the
living conditions of Rome's mythical ancestors and the lifestyle of the
man who governed their own Rome. This contrast was manifest in the
buildings on the Palatine. Not far from the splendid complex built by
Augustus, which included his own house, as well as the temple of Apollo
and the libraries, was a modest rustic construction referred to as the hut
of Romulus.[12]

The historian Dio comments on the prestige derived by Augustus from
this juxtaposition:

[12] Solinus, writing shortly after 200 CE, refers to this building as the *tugurium Faustuli*
(Solinus 1.18). Faustulus was the man who, according to myth, discovered the twins
Romulus and Remus being suckled by the wolf and brought them back to his wife
Acca Larentia. Conon, too, mentions Faustulus (*Diegeseis* 48.7–8 = *FGH* 1 210), as
does the twelfth-century *Mirabilia urbis Romae* under 'palaces', while Propertius
(4.1.9) refers to the hut on the Palatine as the *domus ... Remi*. The Propertius
passage will be discussed below.

The royal residence is called Palatium, not because it was ever decided that this was to be its name, but because Caesar lived on the Palatine and had his military headquarters there, though his residence gained a certain degree of fame from the hill itself too, because Romulus had once lived there. (53.16.5)

The Rome of Romulus was evoked not only by the hut but also by the Lupercal at the foot of the Palatine (the cave where the twins had allegedly been found), the *ficus Ruminalis* beside it (the fig tree under which the wolf suckled them) and the stone walls of *Roma quadrata*, believed to be Romulus' original fortifications (though probably no earlier than the fourth century BCE).[13] Comparisons between Augustus and Romulus may have begun as early as 43 BCE.[14] Indeed, instead of Augustus, Octavian is said to have considered calling himself Romulus (Dio 53.16.6, Suet. *Aug.* 7.2). The proximity of their dwellings reinforced the implication that Augustus was Romulus' heir, the new founder of Rome.

A reference in Varro's *De lingua latina* (5.54.1) suggests Romans of the mid third century BCE associated a structure on the Palatine with Romulus.[15] But the earliest author to suggest the full significance of the hut is Dionysius of Halicarnassus, a Greek writing in the time of Augustus, who says of Rome's founders:

Their life [i.e. that of Romulus and Remus] was the life of herdsmen and they lived by their own labour, mainly on the mountains in huts which they built . . . out of sticks and reeds. One of these, known as the hut of Romulus, remained even to my day on the slope of the Palatine Hill which faces towards the Circus, and it is preserved as holy by those who are responsible for such matters; they add no ornaments to it but if any part of it is injured, either by storms or by the passage of time, they repair the damage and restore the hut as nearly as possible to its former condition. (1.79.11)[16]

---

[13] Cf. Wiseman (1984), 125–8; Balland (1984), 62–6. On Augustus' house in general see Carettoni (1983); Zanker (1988), 51, 93, 207. On the topography of the Palatine see also Wiseman (1981).

[14] When twelve vultures were said to have appeared to Augustus, as he took the auspices – just as they had done to Romulus (Suet. *Aug.* 95.2).

[15] Balland (1984), 59.

[16] Plutarch (*Rom.* 20.4) also gives a very specific location for the hut, apparently referring to a site beside *scalae Caci* (though the text itself is corrupt).

The hut, carefully looked after by the *pontifices*, no doubt conveyed a rather sanitised picture of the life of Rome's earliest inhabitants. Yet the vigilance of those responsible for the hut, remarked on by Dionysius, was certainly necessary; even more than other buildings in Rome, the hut, with its roof of straw, was vulnerable to destruction by fire. Dio mentions two instances of this, both in the time of Augustus and both regarded as portentous. In 12 BCE, following the death of Augustus' associate Agrippa, among other portents: 'Many buildings of the city were destroyed by fire, among them the hut of Romulus which was set ablaze by crows which dropped upon it burning meat from some altar' (54.29.8). Similarly among the portents of 38 BCE, Dio notes that: 'The hut of Romulus was burned as a result of some ritual which the pontifices were performing in it' (48.43.4). Dio's narrative emphasises the hut's significance (its role as a location for the performance of religious rites seems to have increased its liability to fire damage). But so assiduous were the Romans in renovating this holy relic that some version of it was still to be seen on the Palatine in at least the fourth century CE. The *Notitia* (a regionary catalogue of the fourth century) lists under the buildings on the Palatine the *casa Romuli* – the hut of Romulus. Indeed it is the first item on the list for that region of the city.[17]

The hut of Romulus, many times rebuilt, was perhaps as much a fiction as the *mores maiorum* – customs of the ancestors – of which it was the physical symbol. Yet constant renewal of the hut could also function as a demonstration of concern for the preservation of those values with which it was associated.[18] Roman moralists were not overly preoccupied with authenticity. We might compare the attitude revealed by Cicero's complaints in his treatise on the republic about the neglect of Roman institutions.

> nostra vero aetas cum rem publicam sicut picturam accepisset egregiam, sed iam evanescentem vetustate, non modo eam coloribus eisdem, quibus fuerat, renovare neglexit, sed ne id quidem curavit, ut formam saltem eius et extrema tamquam lineamenta servaret.

> The republic our age inherited was like a marvellous painting now fading through the lapse of time. But we failed to restore its colours to

---

[17] Though the twelfth-century *Mirabilia urbis Romae* refers to 'the palace of Romulus near the hut of Faustulus', it is unclear whether the structure referred to is to be identified with the classical 'hut of Romulus'.

[18] Cf. Martial's praise of Domitian for restoring the hut (8.80).

their earlier brightness and we even omitted to maintain its form and
general outlines.   (*Rep.* 5.2)

The authenticity of the materials is not of great concern; Cicero's ideal is
a restored picture with no traces of age.[19]

Livy and other ancient writers identified the Palatine as the site of
Rome's earliest settlement. Modern archaeological investigation has
tended to confirm this view. There are signs that the hill was occupied
from the tenth century BCE. Three hut floors dating back to the eighth
century (when Romulus is supposed to have lived) were found on the
Germalus, the North West of the Palatine, in 1948[20] – though it is not
clear that these are the same remains as those associated by later Romans
with Romulus.

But the version of Roman history evoked by the city of Rome was not
so neat as all this might imply, for the hut of Romulus on the Palatine was
not the only hut of Romulus known to later Romans. From the
Augustan period on, there are references to a hut of Romulus on another
hill, the Capitol. Vitruvius, for instance, commenting on primitive
building techniques, observes:

> in Capitolio commonefacere potest et significare mores vetustatis
> Romuli casa et in arce sacrorum stramentis tecta.

> On the Capitolium the hut of Romulus and on the citadel shrines
> roofed with straw can recall to our minds and make clear the customs
> of antiquity.   (2.1.5)

Other writers, too, refer specifically to this structure on the Capitol.[21] The
latest reference specifically to the Capitoline hut of Romulus is in
Macrobius' *Saturnalia* (1.15.10), written around the turn of the fourth
and fifth centuries. The hut seems to have been located in the *area*

[19] The desire for authenticity of form rather than of materials evident in this and other
Roman texts is in some ways parallel to traditional Shinto practice in Japan, where
temples are regularly rebuilt completely (as Richard Harrison has pointed out to
me). See Harada (1937), 7.

[20] See Momigliano (1989), 63–8. For a detailed discussion of the site see Pensabene
(1990), 86–90.

[21] E.g. elder Seneca *Controv.* 1.6.4 (discussed below); 2.1.5; Conon *Diegeseis* 48 (*FGH*
1, 210). Cf. a military diploma of 78 CE which mentions it as a landmark:
DESCRIPTUM ET RECOGNITUM EX TABULA AENEA QUAE FIXA EST ROMAE IN CAPITOLIO
POST CASAM ROMULI (*CIL* 16.23, final sentence).

Capitolina, that is the sanctuary around the temple of Jupiter Capitolinus.

Earlier I discussed Aeneas' visit to the site of Rome in *Aeneid* 8. Later in the same book, Virgil's description of the shield of Aeneas includes incidents from the future history of Rome. Among these is Manlius' defence of the Capitol against attacking Gauls in the early fourth century BCE:[22]

> in summo custos Tarpeiae Manlius arcis
> stabat pro templo et Capitolia celsa tenebat,
> Romuleoque recens horrebat regia culmo.

> At the top of the shield, Manlius, warden of the Tarpeian
> citadel, was at his post before the temple, defending the
> towering citadel, and there, newly thatched with stiff straw,
> stood the palace of Romulus.   (*Aen.* 8.652–4)

Recens can function as a reference to Vulcan's recent creation of the shield but it can also be read as a reference to a renovation of Romulus' hut in the time of Manlius (reminding us of Dionysius of Halicarnassus' comments on perpetual renewal of the hut).[23] Gransden in his commentary remarks on the effectiveness of the topographical doubling of the hut for Virgil's narrative. The explicit mention of the hut on the Capitol serves to evoke the hut of Romulus on the Palatine, which Evander's hut, also on the Palatine, might be thought to resemble – both the Capitoline hut and that of Evander (at 363) are referred to by the paradoxical term *regia*, 'palace'. Thus Evander the proto-founder of Rome and Romulus the actual founder can be seen as resembling one another in their living conditions and therefore in their virtuous lifestyles. The two Romulean huts merge, the associations of their two sites enriching one another.

This doubling functions elegantly for Virgil but it may seem strange none the less that the Romans should have venerated *two* huts as the humble dwelling of Romulus, the founder of their city.[24] Balland has recently offered an account of the construction of the second hut, that on the Capitol, dating it to the time of Augustus.[25] The building of the hut

---

[22] For a clear discussion of the topographical implications of various versions of the Manlius story, see Wiseman (1979).

[23] Cf. Gransden (1976), *ad loc.* and Balland (1984), 71.

[24] Though such doubling has some parallels in Roman myth – indeed Romulus and Remus may be seen as an example, as Duncan Kennedy has suggested to me. See Alföldi (1974), 164–80.

[25] Other dates have also been suggested. For a discussion of this, see Balland (1984), 73–4.

would have been part of the reordering of the *area Capitolina* of 26–20 BCE.[26] Augustus had already restored the temple of Jupiter Feretrius (a temple on the Capitol allegedly dedicated by Romulus himself).[27] Balland suggests this reinforcement of the links between Romulus and the Capitol may have served to make Augustus' appropriation of the Palatine association with Romulus seem less heavy-handed.[28] Augustus' own project Balland sees as reinforced by writers associated with the emperor (Virgil, Horace, Livy), none of whom refers explicitly to the hut on the Palatine.[29] This is, he suggests, evidence of their tactful concern to avoid a total assimilation of Augustus to Romulus.[30] One might also detect a desire to avoid the upstaging of the Capitol, the religious centre of Rome, by the Palatine.[31] Yet if the Palatine hut were the more familiar, its absence from these texts could also be read as drawing attention to the new regime's doubling of the hut – a concrete instance of the autocratic desire to have Roman history both ways. For a writer to specify any location for a 'hut of Romulus' was to become implicated in the multiple versions of early Roman history which proliferated under the Augustan principate.

But the exact location of the hut is not an obvious concern in many of the ancient texts which refer to it (interestingly no ancient text refers to the fact that there were two huts of Romulus). For many purposes, it did not matter precisely where Romulus lived, just as it did not matter that the hut itself was so often reconstructed. The hut could still function as a vivid symbol of the Roman past. Often the hut was used by writers, such as Valerius Maximus, as a means of celebrating Roman achievement, emphasising the fabulous growth of the city from humble beginnings.[32] The elder Seneca gives this an extra twist:

---

[26] See Gros (1976a), 97.

[27] Balland (1984), 75.

[28] Though, as Denis Feeney has pointed out to me, an attempt to import a Palatine element onto the Capitol could be seen as making the Capitol a more Romulean (and therefore more Augustan) site.

[29] Balland (1984), 66.

[30] Though emphasising differences between Augustus and Romulus could also be subversive. See Hinds' discussion of Ovid's *Fasti* referred to below.

[31] Cf. concerns expressed over the relative neglect of the cult of Jupiter Capitolinus, some of whose functions were taken over by the temples of Apollo and of Mars Ultor (Suet. *Aug.* 91.2 and Zanker (1988), 108).

[32] Cf. Val. Max. 2.8: *disciplina militaris acriter retenta ... ortum ... e parvula Romuli casa totius terrarum orbis fecit columen.* Cf. 4.4.11.

quemcumque volueris revolve nobilem: ad humilitatem pervenies.
quid recenseo singulos, cum hanc urbem possim tibi ostendere? nudi
⟨hi⟩ stetere colles, interque tam effusa moenia nihil est humili casa
nobilius ... potes obiurgare Romanos quod humilitatem suam cum
obscurare possint ostendunt, et haec non putant magna nisi apparuerit
ex parvis surrexisse?

Unroll the family tree of any nobleman you like: you will arrive at low
birth if you go back far enough. Why should I list individuals? I could
use the whole city as my example. Once these hills stood bare – and
within the extensive confines of our walls there is nothing more noble
than a lowly hut ... Can you reproach the Romans? They could
conceal their humble origins but instead they make a display of them
and do not regard all this as great unless it is made obvious that it rose
from a small beginning.   (*Controv.* 1.6.4)

Even anxieties about the nature of individual distinction in an age of
rapid social mobility could be assuaged by appealing to the example of
the city of Rome itself.[33]

For some writers, though, the hut of Romulus was a tired symbol. The
younger Seneca can be found mocking those who make moralising
reference to Romulus' hut. In the consolatory address to his mother on
the occasion of his exile, he writes of the impediments splendid surroundings
may pose to spiritual well-being and continues:

in eam te regionem casus eiecit, in qua lautissimum receptaculum casa
est; ne tu pusilli animi es et sordide se consolantis, si ideo id fortiter
pateris quia Romuli casam nosti.

Has fate cast you into a country where the most luxurious accommo-
dation is a hut? Indeed you show a feeble spirit and comfort yourself
most pitifully, if you bear this bravely only because you know the hut
of Romulus.   (*Helv.* 9.3)

For Seneca, the hut transcends its specifically Roman associations;
Romulus is irrelevant. Instead of evoking the origins of the city of
Rome, a hut represents the life of poverty which is sufficient for all

---

[33] For similar comments on the unimportance of noble ancestry, cf. Sen. *Ep.* 44.1; Juv.
8.272–3.

those, Roman or non-Roman, who have attained true wisdom.[34] Yet this passage also suggests the extent to which the hut of Romulus had become a familiar trope of Roman moralising – a role which must have multiplied the associations called up for all those who visited the lowly structure.

The hut was a live connection with the distant past. By parading their veneration for it, Romans demonstrated the persistence of the virtues of their rustic ancestors even in the vast metropolis of the emperors. Livy, in his description of Roman reactions to the sack of their city by the Gauls, makes the hero Camillus argue, against those who would desert Rome for the empty city of Veii:[35]

si tota urbe nullum melius ampliusve tectum fieri possit quam casa illa conditoris est nostri, non in casis ritu pastorum agrestiumque habitare est satius inter sacra penatesque nostros quam exsulatum publice ire? maiores nostri, convenae pastoresque, cum in his locis nihil praeter silvas paludesque esset, novam urbem tam brevi aedificarunt: nos Capitolio atque arce incolumi, stantibus templis deorum aedificare incensa piget?

If no house in all the city could be put up better or bigger than is the famous hut of our founder, would it not be better to live in huts as shepherds and countrymen do, among our sacred monuments and household gods, than to go out as a people into exile? Our ancestors, refugees and shepherds, when there was nothing but forests and marshes in this region, rapidly built a new city, and are we unwilling, though Capitol and citadel are unharmed and the temples of the gods are still standing, to rebuild what has been destroyed by fire?

(5.53.8)

Camillus' contemporaries should choose to live in huts like the early Romans rather than to abandon the ruins of the city those early Romans founded. In Livy's imagination (as in Virgil's), the hut of Romulus could stand for an earlier, more virtuous Rome even in the early fourth century BCE – though at the same time the Romans of that day, more prosperous

[34] Cf. Sen. *Ep.* 66.3: *potest ex casa vir magnus exire.*
[35] This passage is of some significance for attitudes to the religious topography of Rome under Augustus, which will be discussed in Ch. 2.

and civilised than their founder, are represented as unwilling to live in Romulean simplicity. The pastoral life lived by Romulus and his brother is repeatedly emphasised in references to Romulus' hut. The way of life of Romulus is elided with that of shepherds and country dwellers in Camillus' speech. Though Romulus was the founder of the mighty city of Rome, yet he lived in a Rome which had no urban features – an essentially rustic city.

This was a paradox regularly paraded by Roman moralists. But the nostalgia with which the days of Romulus were regarded by those meditating on the hut could have an edge to it. In Ovid's *Fasti* Mars is made to say: *quae fuerit nostri, si quaeris, regia nati,* | *aspice de canna straminibusque domum*, 'Should you ask what my son's palace was, behold that house of reeds and straw' (3.183–4).[36] The contrast beween the Romulean hut and the Augustan palace, emphasised by the ironic use of *regia* for the hut, was open to a range of readings.[37] Should one approve the new palace as a sign of the city's great increase in power and prosperity since the time of Romulus? Or should one disapprove of it as a sign of how far Romans had come from the simple virtues of Rome's founder? Propertius explicitly links the change from rustic to urban Rome with a change from virtue to avarice: *atque utinam Romae nemo esset dives, et ipse* | *straminea posset dux habitare casa!* | *numquam venales essent ad munus amicae*, 'If only there were no rich men in Rome and even our leader could live in a hut of straw! Then never would our girlfriends be bought for a gift' (2.16.19–21). In juxtaposing his house with the hut of Romulus, Augustus had created a topographical configuration which might be read as emphasising the contrast between himself and Romulus to his own disadvantage.

Ovid's *Fasti* treats Romulus at immense length but presents him as explicitly inferior to Augustus (in particular at 2.137–44): *vis tibi grata fuit, florent sub Caesare leges*, 'You chose the use of force; under Caesar the laws flourish' (141). Yet this too can be seen as subversive, as Stephen Hinds has effectively demonstrated. For Augustus himself, as we have seen, had so strongly identified with the figure of Romulus whom Ovid

---

[36] Cf. also Ovid *Fasti* 5.91–6.
[37] The word *regia* echoes Virgil *Aen.* 8.363 and 654 (both quoted above), thus suggesting an ironic reading of the Virgilian passages, as Stephen Hinds points out to me.

chose to represent as brutal, ignorant and bellicose.[38] However, the most problematic aspect of the Romulus story for Rome's new Romulus was the founder's reputation as a fratricide. Ovid's Romulus is innocent of striking his brother. But as Hinds points out, the death of Remus has uncomfortable prominence in the *Fasti* and Ovid 'chooses to exonerate the primitive king in a way that seems to encourage a measure of continued disquiet about his conduct'.[39]

The hut of Romulus was also, at one time, the hut of Remus. Propertius, in an elegy which evokes an image of early pastoral Rome with many similarities to that conjured up in *Aeneid* 8, includes the hut with a mention of Romulus' brother:

> Hoc quodcumque vides, hospes, qua maxima Roma est,
>   ante Phrygem Aenean collis et herba fuit;
> atque ubi Navali stant sacra Palatia Phoebo,
>   Evandri profugae procubuere boves.
> fictilibus crevere deis haec aurea templa.
>   nec fuit opprobrio facta sine arte casa;
> Tarpeiusque Pater nuda de rupe tonabat,
>   et Tiberis nostris advena murus erat.
> qua gradibus domus ista, Remi se sustulit olim:
>   unus erat fratrum maxima regna focus.

All you see here, visitor, where now stands mighty Rome, before the time of Phrygian Aeneas, was grassy hill. Where stands the Palatine sacred to Apollo of the Ships, lay the cattle of Evander the exile. These golden temples were built for gods of clay and it brought no shame that their dwellings were wrought artlessly. Tarpeian Jupiter used to thunder from the naked rock and the immigrant Tiber was our ancestors' wall. Where stands that house above a flight of steps, was once the house of Remus; a single hearth was all the mighty kingdom of two brothers.   (4.1.1–10)

---

[38] Hinds (1992), esp.127–8, 132–49. Cf. Wallace-Hadrill (1987), esp. 228. On the emphasis given to Romulus in the *Fasti*, see also Barchiesi (1994), 132–65. In the late republic, Romulus had regularly been invoked as a negative examplar, with frequent reference to his brother's murder. Cf. Evans (1992), 87–108.

[39] Hinds (1992),145. On Remus in the *Fasti*, see also Barchiesi (1994), 109–12.

This evocation of Rome then-and-now contains familiar elements – the Capitol now golden, once green; the grazing cattle of Evander; the rock already called Tarpeian before Tarpeia; Apollo; the Tuscan Tiber.[40] And the hut – but this time the hut of Remus.[41] Camps suggests that Remus stands for Romulus here for reasons of metrical convenience.[42] Remus' unsettling presence in this idyllic picture of early Rome should not be so easily explained away. The brother dispossessed and murdered, the act of fratricide always already lurking at the beginning of Roman history, prefiguring the succession of civil wars which, of course, included the one that brought Augustus to power – a reminder of all this in the context of Propertius' Elegies is surely no metrical accident.[43] As for his readers, perhaps they, too, visiting the hut on the Palatine (or the Capitol), sometimes thought not only of Romulus but also of Remus and all that Remus signified.

The hut of Romulus was a sacred place, a fragment of the distant past (or so Romans believed) embedded in a context thickly encrusted with mid and late republican stories about early Rome, overlaid with all the contradictory associations of the Augustan regime. How was it to be read? As a starting-point for contemplation of the humble beginnings of the mighty city, of the virtues of the *maiores* on whose achievements the empire rested, or perhaps of a morally ambiguous contrast between the rustic past and the golden present? If the writings of Livy, Virgil and others could lend new resonance to the hut, the hut, too, with all its varied associations, influenced the ways Roman readers responded to those literary texts.

Topography, for Romans, perhaps played a greater role than chronology in making sense of the past. Past time was conflated and places became

---

[40] The parallels with Virgil are traced by Weeber (1978). For a discussion of various versions of the story of Romulus and Remus see now Wiseman (1995).

[41] What structure Propertius is referring to here is a matter of dispute (charted by Weeber (1978), n.11). Some scholars have suggested the Temple of Quirinus (reconstructed and dedicated by Augustus on the Quirinal in 16 BCE shortly before the poem was written), others the house of Augustus on the Palatine. We might also read this as a reference to the hut of Romulus itself – now standing in the place of the hut of his dispossessed brother. The location *gradibus* would fit with Plutarch's location of the hut of Romulus beside the *scalae Caci* on the Palatine (*Rom.* 20.4). For a more ingenious explication of these lines see Balland (1984), 65–6.

[42] Camps (1965), *ad loc.*

[43] Stephen Hinds and Denis Feeney did not let me get away with ignoring Remus here. Other subversive strands in Propertius Book 4 will be examined in Ch. 2.

vehicles for a kind of non-sequential history (we can have access to Romans' sense of place only through their narratives, but such narratives are often distinctive for their emphasis on the immediacy of the past as experienced through place). Monuments associated with different periods evoked resonant episodes from the Roman past in a pageant which transcended the rigid chronological succession of annalistic records.[44] One might compare the city of Rome, in which buildings of different periods were everywhere juxtaposed, to the funeral of a Roman aristocrat, where living members of the family wore masks to represent prominent figures of previous generations, mingling with one another indifferently across the centuries.[45]

But could all these figures meet without friction? A single family might attempt (not always with success) to impose coherence on its own past, promulgating a single version of its history. The more complex history of the city was harder to control. The stories evoked by a particular place in the city might have different versions. Dupont reminds us of the contradictory stories associated with the *lacus Curtius* in the Forum Romanum.[46] Or the same story might be associated with competing locations. Did Manlius fight off the invading Gauls from the Temple of Jupiter Capitolinus or from the Tarpeian rock?[47] And what of Romulus, Rome's founder? Was he or wasn't he nurtured by a wolf? Was his apotheosis a trick? And, most tellingly, did he kill his own brother? With the civil wars of the first century BCE, culminating in the establishment of an autocratic regime, the story of the fighting brothers, one dying the other acquiring monarchic power, could take on new resonances, some positive, some sinister. For Romans, places might be thought to embody memory, to preserve a reassuringly fixed version of the city's past, but places too, as we have seen, could be rewritten. The two huts of Romulus, with their competing claims to authenticity, were an uncomfortable reminder that Roman history was never simple or uncontested.

---

[44] I have taken the idea of the non-narrative pageant from the suggestive discussion of the Roman calendar in Beard (1987).

[45] The most detailed account of this is Polybius 6.52–4. On the question of how far the right to display ancestral masks was limited see Hopkins (1983), 255–6. Feeney explores the Roman aristocratic funeral as a model for Aeneas' vision of future Romans in Virgil *Aeneid* 6 (1986), 5. See also Burke (1979).

[46] Dupont (1992), 74. Livy 1.12.10; 1.13.5; 7.6.1–6.Cf. Varro *Ling.* 5.148–50.

[47] See Wiseman (1979), 32–50.

CHAPTER

2

The city of gods

Writing on the edge of the empire, the exiled poet Ovid describes Rome itself as the seat of both empire and the gods: *imperii Roma deumque locus* (*Tristia* 1.5.70). The place of empire in the city will be the focus of Chapter 3. In this chapter we shall look at Rome as the home of the gods. Romans, as we have seen, used places as a means of organising perceptions of the past, both mythical and historical. Places also played a vital role in the articulation of Roman religion. The city of Rome above all other sites was for ancient Romans suffused with religious significance. Indeed, the Roman state religion was thought in important respects unable to function without the city. My aim here will be to explore some aspects of what Herbert Cancik has suggestively termed the city's 'sacred landscape' as constituted through a number of Latin literary texts.[1]

The speech Livy gives Camillus in Book 5 of his History presents the cults of the gods of Rome, both indigenous and imported, as vitally linked with particular places in the city. Livy's Camillus argues that Rome itself is indispensable to Roman identity, for it is only in Roman space that Romans can properly carry out the rituals through which their special relationship with the gods is guaranteed. This chapter will examine some of those links between gods and places as they are deployed in Livy, before going on to look at the relationship between place, divinity and Romanness in two other Augustan texts, Propertius' Elegies Book 4 and Ovid's *Fasti*. All three of these authors were writing in the Rome of Augustus, that is to say at a time when Rome's sacred

---

[1] Cancik (1985). Price (1996) stresses the importance of place in Roman religion.

landscape was undergoing a profound transformation. Livy's History in particular was to remain central to the way pagan elite Romans understood their state religion and their city even in late antiquity.[2]

Particular places have ritual significance in virtually all religions. What is striking about Roman texts is the particular interconnections they assert between religion, place and Roman identity. A number of the texts to be examined in this chapter are deeply preoccupied with the question of Rome's essence. Can Rome ever be anywhere other than in Rome? This question is to be connected with a more mundane one, must the empire's capital be in Rome? The final part of the chapter will follow through some strands in the tradition of thought concerned with these issues, looking at their redeployment in later discussions of Rome and Roman identity. Rome was to lose its status as the capital of secular dominion. Yet paradoxically, despite its continuing role as the centre of pagan religious practice in the Roman empire, it was to become capital of the spiritual empire of the Catholic church.

Replacing Rome?

Camillus' speech to his fellow Romans is the culmination of Livy's first pentad.[3] After the humiliation of defeat at Allia at the hands of the Gauls, the Romans had seen their own city besieged and almost taken by their Gallic enemies. In Livy's account, the lower parts of the city are ransacked, elderly senators slaughtered. At the last minute, just as the Romans are poised to hand over a ransom to the Gallic leaders, Camillus, a Roman general who had been forced into exile, intervenes, calling on the Romans to defend their city not with gold but with their swords. The Romans, though weakened by the siege, manage to defeat the Gauls and drive them from Rome. Their city has, however, been devastated.

Scholars have emphasised the various ways in which Livy represents Roman identity as profoundly imperilled in the fifth book of his History.[4]

---

[2] Cf. Liebeschuetz (1979), 89: 'It may well be that the most important long-term effect of the Augustan revival was literary, a reshaping of the religious imagination of the Romans as a result of the religious colouring of Roman literature.'

[3] On the significance of Book 5's structure for Livy's view of Roman history, see Miles, (1986).

[4] See most recently Kraus (1994), esp. 278–82, and Miles (1986).

At crucial moments in the narrative leading up to the Allian defeat, Romans fail to behave like Romans (5.36.1; 5.38.5). Indeed the un-Roman behaviour of the legates leads directly to Rome's involvement in ill-fated conflict with the Gauls. This crisis of Roman identity is symbolised by plans to translate Rome's population to a new site, Veii, a town conquered by the Romans before the Gauls' invasion. The transfer of Rome's population to Veii is put forward not once but twice. After Veii is captured, the tribunes of the plebs are made to propose that half of Rome's population should move to Veii (5.24.4–25; 5.29–30). After Rome itself has been sacked by the Gauls, it is again the tribunes of the plebs who suggest that the entire population of the city should take up residence in Veii (5.49.8; 5.50.8). Camillus, having already saved Rome once by persuading his fellow citizens to withstand the Gauls, saves Rome again by persuading the Romans not to abandon their own city.

The argument for staying in Rome which he is made to develop at greatest length concerns the city's religious significance:

> urbem auspicato inauguratoque conditam habemus; nullus locus in ea non religionum deorumque est plenus: sacrificiis sollemnibus non dies magis stati quam loca sunt in quibus fiant.

> We have a city founded with due augury and auspice, no place within it but is permeated with religious observance and divine presence. Just as the days are fixed for our sacred ceremonies, so too are the places where they are performed.   (5.52.2)

Places in the city are, in religious terms, parallel to days in the calendar. The place and time prescribed for a particular rite are an essential part of that ceremony's meaning and power. In Livy's account of the resumption of Roman good fortune, a key role is played by the story of Fabius, who braves the Gallic besiegers in order to celebrate a family festival on the appointed day in the appointed place, that is on the Quirinal (5.46.2). This incident is also recalled in Camillus' speech (5.52.3–4).

Camillus presents as unthinkable the observance of particular rites anywhere other than in the places where they have traditionally been held (5.52.7). Rome's future successes are implicitly bound up in the proper observance of religious rites and the preservation of religious objects in their allotted places. The cult of Vesta is of vital importance here. The sacred fire in Vesta's temple was not to be permitted to go out; such a failure was felt to portend disaster for Rome. The *pignus imperii* Camillus refers to is the Palladium, said to have been brought by Aeneas from Troy, and kept in Vesta's temple. A key incident in Livy's account of the rehabilitation of Roman character in Book 5, as Kraus has emphasised, is the help offered to the fleeing Vestals by a plebeian family (5.40.5–10). The *sacra*, including the Palladium, are carried from the besieged city to safety (only a true emergency sanctions moving them from their proper place).[5]

Camillus goes on to warn of the danger that the site of Rome, if abandoned, may be appropriated by others who would then make a claim to Roman identity:

> quid? si non Galli hoc sed veteres hostes vestri, Aequi Volscique, faciant ut commigrent Romam, velitisne illos Romanos, vos Veientes esse?

> What if, rather than the Gauls, your old enemies, the Aequi or the Volsci were to move to Rome, would you like it if they were Romans and you the Veientes?   (5.53.7)

Romanness here is presented not as a nebulous, abstract quality but as concretely related to a particular place and imperilled by absence from that place. Further arguments are adduced by Livy, among them the practical advantages of the site of Rome, but also the affection Rome itself inspires in its citizens. In the end, it was especially Camillus' references to religion which served to persuade his audience, according to Livy (5.55.1). The Romans decide to stay. Livy celebrates Camillus as a new founder of Rome.

Scholars since Mommsen have connected the speech Livy gives to Camillus, arguing for the importance of Rome's site, with particular anxieties current in the late republic. Rumours had been circulating shortly before Caesar's assassination that he planned to move the capital either to Alexandria or to Troy (Nicolaus of Damascus *Caesar* 20; Suetonius *Caesar* 79.3). Whatever their basis such rumours seem to have aroused great concern. A few years later in 32 BCE, similar stories were told about another Roman leader; Antony, it was said, planned to move the empire's capital to Egypt (Dio 50.4.1).[6] According to the document

---

[5] Kraus (1994), 276. The *sacra* on which the safety of Rome was thought to depend were at the time Livy was writing understood to be: the Palladium, the image of the mother of the gods, the chariot which had been brought from Veii, the ashes of Orestes, the sceptre of Priam, the veil of Iliona and the sacred shields .

[6] On these rumours see Ceausescu (1976).

alleged by Octavian to be his will, Antony wished to have his remains buried in Alexandria (Dio 50.3.5). Octavian, by contrast, ordering the construction of his own mausoleum on the banks of the Tiber, demonstrated his commitment to Rome's site.[7] For Livy's earliest readers, it would have been difficult not to see his celebration of Camillus' commitment to the physical site of Rome as a positive response to Octavian's well-publicised commitment to the city.

The parallels between Camillus and Augustus go much further than a generalised commitment to the site of Rome, however. Miles has suggestively drawn out the significance of Livy's use of the term *conditor*, 'founder' – applied in his narrative to both Camillus and Augustus. A small number of Roman institutions are ascribed by Livy to individual leaders, whom he designates as *conditores*.[8] The activities of all these individuals, with one exception, are presented as taking place in the period covered by the first pentad of Livy's history (Appius Claudius the decemvir, Brutus, Camillus and all Rome's kings, apart from Tarquinius Superbus, are termed *conditores*). The exception is Augustus, though the term as applied to him occurs within the first pentad, at 4.20.7. Romulus is the greatest of these founders; his work adumbrates that of many of his successors. But Camillus and Augustus stand in a rather different relationship to Romulus from that of the other *conditores*. Both are presented not as creators of new institutions but as renewers of old ones. The contribution of Livy's Camillus, as Miles notes, 'reaffirms allegiance to the physical site of Rome and to the gods attached to that site'.[9] The defeat of the Gauls and re-establishment of Rome in which Camillus plays a crucial part are referred to in the opening chapter of Book 6 of Livy's History as *secunda origine*, Rome's 'second foundation' (6.1.3). Augustus too is presented as a restorer of Rome, in particular Rome's religious identity. Camillus is termed *Romulus ac parens patriae conditorque alter urbis* (5.49.7).[10] Although Augustus did not officially receive the title of *pater patriae* until 2 BCE, the term *pater urbium*, 'father of cities', was applied to him in poetry at least before 23 BCE (Horace *Carm.* 3.24.25).

The chronology offered by Livy's history also suggests an important relationship between Romulus, Camillus and Augustus. Camillus' refoundation of Rome is presented in Livy's narrative as having taken

---

[7] Cf. Kraft (1967).
[8] Miles (1988).
[9] Miles (1988), 200.
[10] On the parallels see Hellegouarc'h (1970), Miles (1986).

place in the 365th year from the original foundation of the city, that is to say in 390 BCE (5.54.5). With inclusive counting, the 365th year from the latter date fell in 27 BCE, the most likely date for the publication of the first five books of Livy's History.[11] Camillus then, in Livy's account, stands exactly midway between Romulus and Augustus.

Religion, for Livy, plays a central part in both the Camillan and the Augustan restorations of Rome.[12] Camillus' speech, as we have seen, strongly emphasises the vital link between religious *pietas* and Roman success. Augustus, earlier in Livy's narrative, is referred to as *templorum omnium restitutorem ac conditorem*, 'the restorer and founder of all our temples' (4.20.7). This aspect of Augustus' activities in Rome is an important part of the context in which Livy's account of Camillus should be viewed. Augustus' own *Res gestae* (in particular, Chapters 19–21) devote much space to the princeps' restoration of a number of existing Roman temples and to his construction of new ones. At 20.4, for instance, he claimed to have restored in one year alone eighty-two temples.

In the late republic there had been some anxieties about religious neglect; Varro's *Antiquitates rerum divinarum* of 47 BCE opens with a dedication to Julius Caesar, exhorting him to remedy the neglect of Roman religion.[13] Cicero too can sometimes be found expressing concern that some Roman rites are falling into disuse (*De haruspicum responsis* 32; *De natura deorum* 1.82). However, the texts, such as Horace's Odes, which place strongest emphasis on the decay of Roman religion are rather later in date.[14] The Augustan regime had a large vested interest in exaggerating the extent to which temples had suffered neglect during the republic's final years.[15] As Gros stresses, the first temples to be restored were not necessarily the most prominent in the city but were rather ones with particular symbolic links to Rome's earliest history: the temple of Jupiter Feretrius (associated with Romulus), that of Victoria (associated with Evander) and that of Saturn (associated with Hercules).[16] These restorations, then, were not simply a matter of improving Rome's

[11] Miles (1986).
[12] On the crucial role of Roman religion in Livy's History, see Liebeschuetz (1967) and (1979), 59–62; Levene (1993), esp. 175–203 on Book 5.
[13] The passage is quoted in the Introduction, above.
[14] Cf. e.g. *Carm.* 3.6.
[15] Cf. Gros (1976a), 21–2; Beard (1994), 736–8.
[16] Gros (1976a), 26. Later on, it seems, Augustus tended to focus rather on new buildings; indeed it seems some ancient Roman temples disappear from the record altogether under Augustus' rule (Gros (1976a), 21).

appearance, nor even of winning back divine favour allegedly alienated
in the last decades of the republic. They constituted a series of calculated
invocations of Roman history and tradition.

Varro's concern with preserving even the smallest and most puzzling
details of Roman religious practice was one we need not assume to have
been shared by many educated Romans. Even Livy, in whose history
religion has a vital place, did not necessarily consult Varro's work
directly.[17] Nevertheless Livy's sense of the importance of Roman religion
and his perception of the religious significance of Roman space were
surely influenced by Varronian ideas. Livy's own writing (which had a far
wider circulation than the technical works of Varro) must have served to
reinforce perceptions of the relationship between place and cult.

The work of Varro (and also of the later antiquarian Verrius Flaccus)
seems also to have strongly influenced decisions made with respect to
Roman temples by the Augustan regime.[18] In the case of Jupiter
Feretrius, for instance, the emperor was said to have consulted extensively
with the learned Atticus on how the temple should be restored (Nepos
Atticus 20). This Augustan 'revival' may be read as an attempt to return
to traditions more or less artificially constituted but perceived as
necessary to the salvation of Rome. In general, Augustus can be seen as
instituting a 'systematic resacralisation' of the city.[19] His programme of
restoration and Livy's first pentad were roughly contemporary; it is not
possible to plot the relationship between them.[20] Rather both should be
seen as emerging from the same cluster of concerns and as serving to
reinforce one another.[21]

Livy's Camillus, then, presides over the refounding of Rome, a

---

[17] Liebeschuetz (1979), 59. See Levene (1993) for an account of the influences on Livy's
treatment of religion.

[18] See Koch (1960), 199–202.

[19] Gros (1976a), 24, 29.

[20] Luce (1965) and Woodman (1988), 128–35, offer arguments dating Livy 1–5 to the
30s BCE. The strong parallels Miles adduces between Augustus and Livy's Camillus
would then imply a significant Livian influence on Augustus.

[21] As Miles comments (1986), 33. Elsewhere Miles suggestively argues that Livy's
account of early Rome may be seen as simultaneously empowering and constraining
the charismatic leader. While change is not always negative, some Roman
institutions are so central to Roman identity and to Roman success that they must
remain unaltered. Camillus' respect for constitutional proprieties is very strict
(1988), 204–8.

refounding profoundly conditioned by Rome's religious aspect. Serres
has suggestively emphasised the link between city destruction and city
foundation, set out at the opening of Livy's History: *Troia capta* is a
necessary preliminary to *Roma condita*.[22] Kraus, developing this point,
explores the relationship between the destruction of Veii, the destruction
of Rome itself and Rome's refounding in Book 5 of Livy's History. Both
Rome and Veii here are in a sense assimilated to Troy, 'the paradigmatic
urbs capta'. Numerous elements in the narrative of the sack of Veii recall
well-known features of the stories associated with the fall of Troy, as
scholars have noted.[23] Kraus observes a number of implicit parallels
between the sack of Troy and Livy's account of the sack of Rome by the
Gauls, later in Book 5. Interest in Troy as the ancestor of Rome was
already aroused at the time Livy was writing, in particular, by the claims
on the part of Julius Caesar and Augustus himself to be descended from
the Trojan Aeneas.[24] Troy, Kraus suggests, is central to the Roman
identity crisis which is presented as inspiring Camillus' speech. The Gallic
sack is a critical moment for Rome; if the Romans follow through the
Trojan analogy and leave their sacked city, then Rome will be finished.
Instead, she suggests, the Romans are presented as moving beyond their
Trojan phase, keeping hold only of the positive parts of their Trojan
inheritance. Indeed Rome could not be Rome without some part of Troy,
for it was the Palladium, brought to Italy from the ruins of Troy by
Aeneas, which was held to be the guarantee of Rome's future. When
Varro, in the dedication of the *Antiquitates rerum divinarum* (quoted in
the Introduction above), sought to invoke critical moments in the history
of Roman religion, he chose Aeneas saving the Penates from Troy and,
in the third century, the rescue of the *sacra* (including the Trojan
Palladium) from the burning temple of Vesta by the *pontifex maximus*
Metellus.

   The end of Livy Book 5 describes the rebuilding of Rome in the wake
of the Gallic sack. The Romans were in a great hurry to rebuild, he
writes, and for this reason there was no order to the new city, so that
forma . . .urbis sit occupatae magis quam divisae similis, 'the arrangement
of the city resembles that of a place taken over rather than portioned

[22] Serres (1991), 38–9.
[23] Although Book 2 of Virgil's *Aeneid* was probably not yet published when Livy
    composed this part of his History, it is likely that the authors used a common source.
[24] See Evans (1992), 42–57 and Gruen (1993), 6–51.

out' (5.55.5). *Occupata* here may be read as evoking Rome's recent
occupation by the Gauls. Kraus draws our attention to Tacitus' reading
of this Livian episode, which the later author makes use of in his
account of the destruction of Rome in the Neronian fire and the city's
subsequent rebuilding (*Ann.* 15.43.1–5). Tacitus' account presents Nero's
fire as worse than the Gallic sack, for it causes the destruction of
monuments witnessing the origins of Rome.[25] Rome is then rebuilt;
large areas in the centre of the city are taken over for Nero's Domus
Aurea. Nero's appropriation of the city is like that of a foreign enemy.
Rome has been alienated. Certainly Nero's contemporaries seem to
have seen parallels between the emperor's building projects and the sack
of Rome by the Gauls. Suetonius recalls joking verses proposing that
citizens should move to Veii, if Nero's house takes over Rome (Suet.
Nero 39.2). For Romans, whose views of their own early history were
profoundly coloured by Livy's work, Veii remained in symbolic terms a
place to go to when Rome itself was occupied by an enemy or
devastated beyond repair.

Rome's founding and refounding in Livy's History are preceded by
destruction, of Troy, then of Rome itself. After the civil wars which
brought the end of the Roman republic, Rome lay again in ruins – at least
metaphorically. According to Augustus, Antony, his rival, had proposed
leaving Rome and making another city the empire's capital. Augustus
chose to identify himself with Rome, affirming his commitment to the city
through an unparalleled programme of building work. Thus Augustus
too might figure himself, according to the Livian formula, as Rome's
refounder. This version, like the Romulean and Camillan ones, depended
on a city's earlier destruction – *Roma capta* becomes *Roma (re)condita*.

Elegiac aetiologies

Augustan appropriations of Roman time, Roman space, Roman religion
and Roman history were inextricably connected. This interrelationship is
taken up in other Augustan texts besides Livy's History. Propertius'
fourth book of Elegies, published after 16 BCE, and Ovid's *Fasti*,
probably written between 5 and 8 CE, also offer suggestive readings of
the Augustan city. At the outset of his fourth book, Propertius promises:

[25] Cf. Rouveret (1991), 3067–8.

sacra diesque canam et cognomina prisca locorum, 'I shall sing of rituals, and days and the ancient names of places' (4.1.69). Ovid, leaving the narration of the princeps' military activities to others, he claims, sets out to tell of *Caesaris aras / et quoscumque sacris addidit ille dies*, 'Caesar's altars and the festivals he has added to the sacred list' (*Fasti* 1.13–14). Both these formulations link time, place and the gods. Here, as in Livy, the contexts of Roman cults are intrinsic to their identities. In different ways, both these works can be seen as engaging with definitions of Rome; the interplay of cults is constitutive of the identity of Rome itself – though, as we saw in Chapter 1, the city as written by Propertius or Ovid may not always offer a reassuring confirmation of Roman identity.

When they came to write directly about the city, both these poets were already known as writers of love elegy – a genre of poetry associated with resistance to engagement with public concerns. Yet both poets chose to use elegiac couplets to write about Rome – a choice which necessarily engenders some generic tension, as scholars have emphasised.[26] The fourth book of Propertius' Elegies presents itself as moving on from the narrowly elegiac world of his previous books. Now his song will be devoted to serving his country: *hoc patriae serviet omne meae* (4.1.60). The elegies in this book interweave more obviously public themes relating to Roman religion and Roman history with poems of love, though as recent critics have pointed out the two elements are not clearly separable; specific Roman locations are integral to 4.8, a poem primarily concerned with an argument between the poet and his mistress, while Propertius' treatment of the legend of Tarpeia examines at length her erotic feelings for Tatius. A number of cults and places in Rome are dealt with in this book: the god Vertumnus (4.2), the Tarpeian rock (4.4), the Palatine temple of Apollo (4.6), the Ara Maxima (4.9), the temple of Jupiter Feretrius (4.10). The programmatic first elegy clearly situates this project in the context of the Alexandrian aetiologising of Callimachus.[27] Propertius' treatment of his aetiological subject is organised topographically; the opening survey of Rome in 4.1 (echoing Aeneas' tour of the site of Rome in Virgil *Aeneid* 8, as we saw in Chapter 1) is supplemented by five treatments of specific landmarks in the city. The larger part of my

---

[26] De Brohun (1994), 42–5 on Propertius; Hinds (1992), 82–111 and Barchiesi (1994), 44–57 on *Fasti*. Herbert-Brown, by contrast, sees Ovid's choice of metre as unproblematic (1994), 2–8, 45–7.

[27] On the use of Callimachean aetiology by both Propertius and Ovid see Miller (1982).

discussion of Propertius will not be concerned directly with his treatment of Roman divinities. The other aspects of Propertius 4 considered here are, however, of particular relevance to more general questions of Roman identity discussed in the present chapter, most notably Rome's relationship to Veii and to Troy.

The Rome celebrated by Propertius is marked as the Rome of Augustus. Two of the five places he treats in detail had strong connections with the princeps. The temple of Palatine Apollo was built by Augustus and dedicated in 28 BCE; Propertius in 4.6 presents the construction as a thank-offering for assistance received from Apollo in the defeat of Antony and Cleopatra at Actium.[28] Most of the poem is devoted to celebrating Augustus' victory. *Caesaris in nomen ducuntur carmina: Caesar | dum canitur, quaeso Iuppiter, ipse vaces*, 'Songs are sung to honour Caesar: while Caesar is sung, I ask that you too, Jupiter, listen' (4.6.14–15).[29] This poem inevitably recalls an earlier treatment by Propertius of the same place (poems 2.31 and 32, presented as a single poem in Goold's edition). The earlier work, however, seems to incorporate a description of the portico associated with the temple of Apollo into a lament about the bad behaviour of the poet's mistress. The poet does not trust her to linger in the portico of Apollo's temple (2.32.7–8) – a sentiment not wholly flattering to the champion of morality responsible for the building's construction.

The temple of Jupiter Feretrius, Rome's earliest temple, according to Livy (1.10) and built by Romulus himself, had, as we saw above, been restored by Augustus. Romulus is celebrated in Propertius' poem as the *urbis virtutisque parens*, 'the father of Rome and of virtue' (4.10.17), a phrase recalling Augustus' still unofficial title *pater patriae*. Yet the poem says nothing directly about Augustus' restoration of the temple and might, from another perspective, be read as a reminder of a somewhat embarrassing episode in recent Roman history. Associated with this temple were the *spolia opima*, won when a Roman commander killed the enemy general. Propertius tells of the three occasions in the distant past on which the *spolia opima* had been won. In 29 BCE, Marcus Licinius Crassus, a proconsul, had succeeded in killing the king of the Bastarnae in single combat. He, however, was not awarded the *spolia opima*, on the

[28] Actually, the temple had been vowed in 36 BCE during the war with Sextus Pompeius (Dio 49.15.5).
[29] On the ambivalence of this poem's praise of Augustus, see Connor (1978).

grounds that, since his power was derived from Octavian, he was not a supreme commander (Dio 51.24). The princeps' military primacy was not to be challenged, even if that meant reinterpreting some republican traditions.

Propertius Book 4 presents the poet as the Roman Callimachus, eager to celebrate Rome: *moenia namque pio coner disponere versu*, 'in loyal verse would I seek to set forth those walls' (4.1.57). The adjective *pius*, along with references to Aeneas earlier in this poem, has been read as evoking the recently published *Aeneid* – a signal of Propertius' claim to emulate Virgil. Yet Propertius' undertaking to celebrate Rome in high-flown verse can be read as not altogether complimentary to Aeneas' alleged descendant, as we have already seen. Poem 4.1 expresses some nostalgia for days before Rome had *externos deos* – an ironical sentiment given that even Rome's Penates were held to have come with Aeneas from Troy. This implicit privileging of indigenous deities is further undercut by the choice of Vertumnus as the subject of 4.2. This slippery deity is not Roman but Tuscan: *Tuscus ego et Tuscis orior*, 'a Tuscan am I and from the Tuscans risen' (4.2.3). The Tuscan is incorporated into Rome; Vertumnus celebrates the Vicus Tuscus, named, he claims, as a reward for services rendered by the Tuscans (4.2.49–50). Rome for Vertumnus is a 'pleasing city' (4.2.60). Yet still this deity seems distanced from Rome, observing the activities of the Romans with a degree of detachment.[30]

Propertius' own Romanness is not altogether straightforward either, for he also emphasises his loyalty to another place, Assisi in Umbria, where he was born. *Umbria Romani patria Callimachi!* 'Umbria, homeland of Rome's Callimachus!' (4.1.64). There is a tension between the *moenia* of Rome (57) and the *muros* of Assisi (66), whose reputation will be enhanced, the poet hopes, by his genius. Cicero in the *De legibus* presented his feelings for Arpinum, his birthplace, and Rome, his official fatherland, as fully compatible (2.5). Propertius' treatment of recent Roman history suggests rather the conflicting sentiments that might be engendered by such a dual allegiance; the most extended treatment of Umbria in Propertius' earlier work, the final poem in Book 1, recalled a kinsman killed in the Perusine war. The end of a poem or the final poem in a book was traditionally used to highlight the poet's own literary identity. Propertius uses this prominent location to bring up the recent

[30] Hardie (1992), 74–5.

civil war, a war which had reopened many of the conflicts between different regions of Italy and between Romans and Italians (as well as bringing Augustus to power).

Troubling too is the repeated link in Propertius' writing between Rome's foundation and expansion and bloodshed, especially the bloodshed of civil strife (compare, too, Propertius' use of Remus, discussed in Chapter 1). Poem 4.1 measures Rome's rise against the decline of surrounding towns, Bovillae, Fidenae, Alba (33–6): *et, qui nunc nulli, maxima turba Gabi*, 'and Gabii, now with not a soul, but then thronging with people'. This comparison can hardly be neutral; the flourishing of Rome has been at the expense of other places in Italy. Poem 4.10, as we have seen, tells the history of the temple of Jupiter Feretrius. The second winner of the *spolia opima* was Cossus, who killed Tolumnius of Veii and captured the city (Propertius' version of the story is somewhat different from that to be found in Livy). From a celebration of Roman success, the poem shifts to a contemplation of Rome's defeated enemy:

> heu Veii veteres! et vos tum regna fuistis,
>   et vestro positast aurea sella foro:
> nunc intra muros pastoris bucina lenti
>   cantat, et in vestris ossibus arva metunt.

> Alas for ancient Veii! You too ruled widely then and a golden throne stood in your forum. Now within your walls the lazy shepherd sounds his pipe and harvests are gathered among your bones.   (4.10.27–30)

The destruction of Veii for Propertius is brought about by Romans spilling Italian blood (4.10.38) – a prelude perhaps to the Social War and civil wars, which had torn Italy apart in the recent past.

Propertius' picture of Veii, transformed from a flourishing city into a rustic idyll (though one sinisterly underlain by human remains), might also be read as recalling the picture of Rome-before-Rome presented in his first elegy. Rome itself has undergone a reverse transformation from rustic landscape to glittering city. But we may wonder if the destruction of other cities which has formed an essential part of Rome's growth may not also be read as portending a possible future for Rome. Veii is of particular significance here. The account of the fall of Veii in Livy's History is not followed in detail by Propertius, but the Livian narrative, examined earlier in this chapter, had surely served to assert an important relationship between Rome and Veii. Veii in Livy almost becomes Rome.

Might Rome some day come near to becoming Veii? Propertius' Elegies, in particular those of Book 4, open up fissures in the solid, confident Roman identity projected both by Augustus' building projects and (at least on some readings) by Virgil's epic.

While Propertius' treatment of Rome approaches the city topographically, Ovid chooses the Roman calendar as his organising scheme. Ovid composed his poem at around the same time as was published an 'official' version of the Augustan calendar (incorporating the princeps' new festivals), which seems to have been largely the work of the scholar Verrius Flaccus, a freedman of the emperor.[31] Recent studies have suggestively examined the treatment of time in Ovid's *Fasti*, exploring the means by which the poet engages with Augustus' ideological appropriation of the calendar.[32] Yet while time is the organising principle of the *Fasti*, places also have an important part to play in Ovid's poem. Gros and others have drawn attention to the intimate relationship between Augustus' transformation of the calendar and his transformation of the city.[33] Temples restored by Augustus, for instance, were in many cases given new foundation days, ones with a particular significance for the princeps and his relatives. Out of the twenty-eight temples restored between 38 BCE and 17 CE where information is available, fourteen were given a new *dies natalis*. Six temples in the Campus Martius originally constructed by triumphant generals of the republic now celebrated their foundation on 23 September, Augustus' birthday – a prelude to the monopolisation of triumphs by the imperial family after 19 BCE.[34] It was not possible, then, to consider the organisation of Roman time without engaging also with the spatial context through which Roman time was articulated.

The deity who presides over the beginning of Ovid's *Fasti* is Janus.[35] The two-headed god, looking at once to the past and to the future, speaks

---

[31] Wallace-Hadrill (1987), 227–8.

[32] Beard (1987), Wallace-Hadrill (1987), Feeney (1992), Barchiesi (1994) and Herbert-Brown (1994). Feeney (1992) emphasises that many of the most important Augustan dates fall in the second half of the year, the months not covered by the *Fasti*. Indeed all forward references to dates later in the year are to two months, August (the month which should have been of greatest interest to Augustus) and December, the final month of the year.

[33] Gros (1976a), in particular 31–6.

[34] Gros (1976a), 29–32.

[35] On Janus' role in the *Fasti*, see Hardie (1991) and Barchiesi (1994), 218–25. Both these scholars also explore the implications of Ovid's stress on Janus' double nature.

from his temple between the Forum Romanum and the Forum Julium
(1.257–8). From the arch between the two fora, a statue of Janus looks
toward both places; the reader may feel tempted to identify the Forum
Romanum with Rome's past and the Forum Julium with Rome's future.
Janus is the god of doorways. Every door, he points out, looks in two
directions: *omnis habet geminas hinc atque hinc, ianua frontes, | e quibus
haec populum spectat, at illa Larem*, 'Every door has two faces, one this
side, one the other. From these the door looks on one side towards the
people, on the other to the household gods' (135–6). In this perspective, if
the Forum Romanum is the place of the Roman people, the Forum
Iulium appears as the site of Rome's hearth-gods, who turn out to be the
Iulii (Augustus had closely associated himself with the city's Lares, as
Ovid later emphasises at *Fasti* 5.129–46). The lengthy section on Janus
culminates with the god's speech in celebration of the peace and victory
brought by the Augustan regime – peace marked by the closing of the
doors of Janus' temple (1.279–88).

Yet the apparently deferential project of a poem on the Roman
calendar is shot through with subversive – or at least playful – elements, as
many scholars have noted. Ovid insists on the doubleness of Janus'
identity: *Iane biformis* (89), *ancipiti mirandus imagine Ianus* (95). There is a
sense in which Rome too has a double identity in Ovid's poem.
Comparisons are drawn between early Rome and contemporary Rome,
when, in response to a question from the narrator, Janus is made to talk
about the role of money in his own festival: *hic ubi nunc Roma est,
incaedua silva virebat, | tantaque res paucis pascua bubus erat*, 'Here where
now is Rome, virgin woods flourished and the seat of a mighty city was
pasture to cattle' (1.243–4) – a trope familiar to the Roman reader from
the work of Virgil, Tibullus and Propertius. In Ovid's Janus-narrative the
contrast is not perhaps so great as it seems. Earlier, Janus had been made
to comment on the continuity between early Rome and the present, a
continuity which relates not to Roman virtue but to Roman vice. Even in
earliest times when Saturn reigned, virtually everyone had a weakness for
money: *vix ego Saturno quemquam regnante videbam, | cuius non animo
dulcia lucra forent*, 'Even when Saturn reigned, I scarcely saw a soul who
did not in his heart find money sweet' (193–4). In earlier days, he is made
to comment, people gave copper coins, now gold is thought more
propitious. The new coin has vanquished the old. Janus continues with
characteristic ambivalence to the simplicity of life in early Rome:
laudamus veteres, sed nostris utimur annis: | mos tamen est aeque dignus

uterque coli, 'We praise the old days but enjoy our own; both ways are just as worthy to be kept' (225–6). Janus is perhaps constitutionally incapable of viewing anything from a single perspective. His double view of Rome, having it both ways, could be seen as dangerously close to the contradictory Augustan urge to celebrate both simple early Rome and the glittering, powerful city, transformed into a monumental capital by the princeps.

The dual focus of the *Fasti* on early Rome and Augustan Rome, to the virtual exclusion of the intervening centuries, has been noted by scholars. Ovid returns repeatedly in the *Fasti* to comparisons between Rome in the distant past and Rome in the present. Later in Book 1, for instance, he evokes the rustic landscape of Rome's future site in the time of Evander (1.499–543). Evander's mother the nymph Carmentis, arriving by boat with her son: *fluminis illa latus, cui sunt vada iuncta Tarenti, | aspicit et sparsas per loca sola casas,* 'sees the riverbank, the spot now next to Tarentum's pool, and a few isolated cottages' (1.501–2). The woods and lonely pastures of the site of Rome before the establishment of the city by Romulus and Remus are alluded to at 3.71–2: *iam, modo quae fuerant silvae pecorumque recessus, | urbs erat* , 'Now, where recently there had been nothing but woods and the grazing places of sheep, there was a city.' Rustic Rome as Evander saw it is again recalled at 5.93–4: *hic, ubi nunc Roma est, orbis caput, arbor et herbae, | et paucae pecudes et casa rara fuit,* 'Here, where now is Rome, the capital of the world, were trees and grass and a few cattle and some cottages.' Later in the same book, the river Tiber is made to remember pastoral Rome: *haec loca desertas vidi sine moenibus herbas: | pascebat sparsas utraque ripa boves,* 'I saw these parts when there was nothing but lonely grasslands – no walls – and a few oxen grazed on the river banks' (5.639–40). The Rome of woodland, pasture, a few cattle and a scattering of rustic huts is becoming almost too familiar. We might be tempted to read this as a *reductio ad absurdum* of the repeated Augustan topos of rustic Rome and the Rome of the princeps.

One of the most extended evocations of early Rome comes in Book 6. The narrator is surprised to see a matron walking barefoot near the Via Nova. He then encounters an old woman, who addresses the following words to him:

> hoc ubi nunc fora sunt, udae tenuere paludes;
>   amne redundatis fossa madebat aquis.
> Curtius ille lacus, siccas qui sustinet aras,
>   nunc solida est tellus, sed lacus ante fuit.

qua Velabra solent in Circum ducere pompas,
  nil praeter salices cassaque canna fuit;
saepe suburbanas rediens conviva per undas
  cantat et ad nautas ebria verba iacit.
nondum conveniens diversis iste figuris
  nomen ab averso ceperat amne deus.
hic quoque lucus erat iuncis et harundine densus
  et pede velato non adeunda palus.
stagna recesserunt et aquas sua ripa coercet,
  siccaque nunc tellus: mos tamen ille manet.

This place now occupied by the fora was once sodden
marshland; a ditch flowed with waters from the river in flood.
The lacus Curtius, now the solid base of dry altars, used to be
a real lake. Where they lead the processions through the
Velabrum to the Circus there was nothing but willows and
empty cane. Often a partygoer returning by suburban
waterway would sing and offer drunken jokes to the sailors.
That god had not yet derived his name (fitting for one who
changes shape) from turning back the river. Here too there
was a grove thick with reeds and rushes and you could not
cross the marsh in your shoes. The pools have receded and
the waters lie within their banks. The ground is dry now but
the custom remains.   (*Fasti* 6.401–14)

It is the custom for Romans to go barefoot in this part of the city, she
says, because it was once marshland. This Ovidian episode is in many
ways curious. Here is an aetiology evoking not a great hero of early
Rome but a drunken partygoer, exchanging jokes with sailors on the site
of the Roman Forum. No other ancient text mentions the custom of
going barefoot in this part of the city. It is tempting to read this episode as
a deliberate absurdity. We might also wonder whether the purpose of the
aetiology is not to parody the repeated evocations of early Rome found
in other Augustan poets (as well as in Livy), which made numerous
references to the marshy state of what was to become the centre of the
city. The mention of Vertumnus here serves to evoke in particular
Propertius Book 4, where, as we have seen, the first landmark to be
treated in detail is the statue of Vertumnus. Indeed, Ovid at 410 echoes

one of the etymologies of the god's name offered in Propertius' poem (while at the same time suggesting that the god's tendency to metamorphose is a more plausible reason for his name).[36] But who is the mysterious old lady? Barchiesi offers the attractive suggestion that she is none other than Vertumnus himself, who, in Ovid's *Metamorphoses* (14.654–6), is noted for his ability to transform himself into many guises, including that of a loquacious old woman.

The narrator of the *Fasti* places his encounter with the barefoot matron on the occasion of the festival of the goddess Vesta. Vesta is referred to in a number of contexts in the *Fasti*. These passages play a vital role in Ovid's articulation of Augustus' status in relation to the divine.[37] Virgil had already presented Vesta as a Trojan goddess, brought to Italy by Aeneas (*Aeneid* 2.296). Ovid stresses her Trojan origin and presents her as even more closely connected with the Julii, indeed as related to them. Augustus had become Pontifex Maximus in 12 BCE. Ovid writes of the anniversary of Augustus' assumption of the pontificate:

> ignibus aeternis aeterni numina praesunt
>   Caesaris: imperii pignora iuncta vides.
> di veteris Troiae, dignissima praeda ferenti,
>   qua gravis Aeneas tutus ab hoste fuit,
> ortus ab Aenea tangit cognata sacerdos
>   numina: cognatum, Vesta, tuere caput!
> quos sancta fovet ille manu, bene vivitis, ignes:
>   vivite inexstincti, flammaque duxque, precor.

> The eternal divinity of Caesar presides over the eternal flame.
> Close by you can see the pledges of empire. O gods of ancient
> Troy, most worthy prize to him who bore you – your weight
> kept Aeneas safe from the enemy – a priest from Aeneas' line
> handles you as kindred divinities. O Vesta, keep safe the head
> of your kinsman! Under the care of his sacred hand, you
> flourish, fires. Live undying flame and leader too, I pray!

> (3.421–8)

---

[36] On the relationship between the two passages, see Barchiesi (1994), 175–8.

[37] As has been recently emphasised by both Barchiesi (1994), 114–17, 127–9, 191–201 and Herbert-Brown (1994), 66–73 – though their observations lead to very differing conclusions.

As a scion of Troy, Augustus is related to the Trojan goddess. As Aeneas' descendant, he has an especially privileged relationship with the divinities his ancestor rescued from Troy. In Ovid's poem, we find for the first time descriptions of the Pontifex Maximus as the priest of Vesta (3.697–702).[38] 'Augustus had taken over the *penates publici* brought by Aeneas to Rome and the hearth of Rome itself as his personal, dynastic, divine right ... Only a Caesar could be Pontifex Maximus.'[39] Augustus' connection was most graphically expressed by the incorporation of a shrine of Vesta into his Palatine residence. At 4.949–54, Ovid celebrates the anniversary of this event: *cognati Vesta recepta est | limine* 'Vesta is received into the home of her kinsman.' Here too, then, Augustus transformed both Rome's ritual calendar and the city's sacred landscape. As Barchiesi has emphasised, Ovid's treatment of Vesta lays much stress on the importance of her original temple and on the fact that she is not to be seen or touched by men. Several mythological episodes in the *Fasti* deal disapprovingly with male characters who make aggressive sexual advances to the pure goddess. Augustus' handling of Vesta, his incorporation of her cult into his own house, may also be read in sexual terms, as a violation of the goddess central to Roman well-being.[40]

In Book 6, immediately after the encounter discussed above, Ovid reverts to the festival of Vesta and gives an account of how the Palladium (now kept in Vesta's temple) came to Rome, and of Metellus' rescue of the *sacra*, when the temple of Vesta was in flames. A prophecy addressed to the Trojans is placed in the mouth of Apollo, emphasising the powerful talismanic qualities of the Palladium:

'aetheriam servate deam, servabitis urbem:
    imperium secum transferet illa loci.'
servat et inclusam summa tenet Ilus in arce,
    curaque ad heredem Laomedonta redit.
sub Priamo servata parum: sic ipsa volebat,
    ex quo iudicio forma revicta sua est.

---

[38] As Herbert-Brown notes. See too Price (1996). Here used with reference to Augustus, the term 'priest of Vesta' is also used with reference to earlier holders of the priesthood, Julius Caesar (5.573) and Metellus. The latter was said to have saved the *sacra* from fire (6.437–54). This retrojection Herbert-Brown reads as serving to legitimate Augustus' appropriation of Vesta (1994), 71.

[39] Herbert-Brown (1994), 72.

[40] Barchiesi (1994), 191–201.

seu genus Adrasti, seu furtis aptus Ulixes,
    seu fuit Aeneas, eripuisse ferunt;
auctor in incerto, res est Romana: tuetur
    Vesta quod assiduo lumine cuncta videt.

'Keep the etherial goddess well and you shall keep your city
well; for when she moves she takes with her imperial sway.'
Ilus looks after her and keeps her shut in the highest citadel
and this charge passes to his heir Laomedon. Under Priam
she was neglected. Such indeed was her will, once her beauty
had been spurned in the contest. Some say she was taken by
the son of Adrastus, some by Ulysses, skilled at theft, others
that it was Aeneas. Whoever took her, now she is Roman.
Vesta guards her, for she watches over all with her unfailing
light.   (*Fasti* 6.427–36)

Watched over by Vesta, the Palladium is within the preserve of Vesta's
priest, as Ovid has termed him, Augustus.[41] The Palladium is here, too,
celebrated as a guarantee of Rome's safety (though Aeneas' role here, in
contrast to Book 3, is rather played down). In Ovid's *Fasti*, as in the
writing of Livy and Propertius, Rome's foundation and flourishing are
presented as profoundly implicated in the fall of Troy.

Roman Troy − Trojan Rome

Virgil, in the final book of the *Aeneid*, had made Juno concede that Rome
might flourish but only on certain conditions:

sit Latium, sint Albani per saecula reges,
sit Romana potens Itala virtute propago:
occidit occideritque sinas cum nomine Troia.

Let Latium be and the Alban kings down through the years.
Let there be the Roman race, strong with Italian manliness,
so long as you leave Troy and the Trojan name, now
perished, to remain so.   (*Aeneid* 12.826–8)

---

[41] Koch notes that the Palladium, little emphasised in the *Aeneid*, appears to acquire
significance in Roman literature only after 12 BCE, when Augustus became *pontifex
maximus* (1960), 146.

For the goddess, a condition of Rome's flourishing is that, although successor to Troy, it will not assume a Trojan identity. Horace makes Juno pronounce Rome doomed, should any attempt be made to revive Troy:

> sed bellicosis fata Quiritibus
> hac lege dico, ne nimium pii
>   rebusque fidentes avitae
>   tecta velint reparare Troiae.
> Troiae renascens alite lugubri
> fortuna tristi clade iterabitur,
>   ducente victrices catervas
>   coniuge me Iovis et sorore.

> But the fortune I tell for the warlike Romans is on these terms: let them not, too dutiful and too confident of themselves, seek to repair the roof of their ancestral Troy. Should Troy rise once more, the same wretched fate, portended by ill-omened fowl, will visit her again. I myself, sister and wife of Jove, shall lead the conquering forces.
>
> (*Carm.* 3.3.57–64)

Rome and Troy cannot coexist for these Augustan writers.[42] The logic of this is brought out in Propertius 4.1.87, where Cassandra is made to prophesy: *Troia, cades et Troica Roma resurges!* 'Troy, you will fall and rise again as Trojan Rome!' It is precisely because Rome is in a sense Troy that Troy cannot rise again without ruining Rome.

Rome, as Troy's successor, displaces Troy, subsuming its gods and its glory. Yet this story could also serve to reinforce an anxiety among Romans that Rome might suffer a similar fate. Troy itself is repeatedly presented as having the power to displace Rome, to reclaim its own identity. Stories current in the time of Julius Caesar, as we saw above, suggested he wished to transfer the site of the empire's capital to Troy, a city closely associated with the Julii.[43] Lucan, in his *Bellum civile*, explores the relationship between Rome and Troy in an extended description of a visit by Julius Caesar to the site where Troy had once been (9.950–99). Caesar invokes the gods, once rescued from burning

[42] Ceausescu (1976), 87–8.
[43] Cf. Ceausescu (1976), 84–6.

Troy and now in Rome, promising that they will be restored to their original dwellings in a rebuilt Troy:

> Di cinerum, Phrygias colitis quicumque ruinas,
> Aeneaeque mei, quos nunc Lavinia sedes
> servat et Alba, lares, et quorum lucet in aris
> ignis adhuc Phrygius, nullique aspecta virorum
> Pallas, in abstruso pignus memorabile templo,
> gentis Iuleae vestris clarissimus aris
> dat pia tura nepos et vos in sede priore
> rite vocat. date felices in cetera cursus,
> restituam populos; grata vice moenia reddent
> Ausonidae Phrygibus, Romanaque Pergama surgent.

> Gods of the ashes, who dwell among the ruins of Troy, household gods of my ancestor Aeneas, now kept by Lavinium and Alba, whose altars glow still with a Trojan flame, and Pallas, whose aspect is forbidden to all men, a famous pledge concealed within a temple, the most famed son of the Julian clan makes pious gifts of incense on your altars and with due rites invokes you in your former home. Grant good fortune for the rest of my undertakings and I shall restore your people. With glad reciprocation, the Italians will rebuild walls for the people of Troy and a Roman Troy shall rise.   (9.990–9)

Julius Caesar's necromantic invocation of the gods of Troy makes clear his personal connection with the city. Indeed, Lucan's Caesar thus makes clear his perverse desire to appropriate Roman history as his own – a desire which contrasts strangely with Caesar's alleged ignorance of the physical and epic topography of Troy.[44] Readers familiar with the passages from Virgil and Horace quoted above might be expected to link the revival of Troy with disaster for Rome itself. Lucan, like Livy, presents the divinities of the city as the key to the city's identity. Troy and Rome cannot coexist because each depends for its existence on the same divinities, the Penates, the Palladium and Vesta, who cannot be in two places simultaneously. Rome itself is both Troy and not-Troy, while Troy is a kind of anti-Rome (perhaps a global equivalent to the Italian

---

[44] Cf. Feeney (1991), 294–5; Martindale (1993), 49–52; Hardie (1993), 107.

anti-Rome of Veii). And it is the Caesars who have the power to make
Rome into Troy or vice versa.

The location of Rome is problematised in other ways elsewhere in
Lucan's epic. The speech Livy gives to Camillus, was, I have suggested, a
text central to ancient Roman perceptions of the city's identity. In Book
5, Lucan makes one of the exiled senators accompanying Pompey refer to
Camillus in a discussion of Roman identity.[45] These members of the
senate have come together far away from the city. Can they still
constitute the senate of Rome? Lentulus argues: *Tarpeia sede perusta* |
Gallorum facibus Veiosque habitante Camillo | *illic Roma fuit*, 'When the
Tarpeian citadel was burnt out by the torches of the Gauls and Camillus
dwelt at Veii, Rome was at Veii' (5.27–9). The logic of Camillus' speech in
Livy's narrative is here completely subverted. Rome is not a place, Rome
is not buildings (at this point in Lucan's account the city itself is held by
Caesar). Rather Roman identity depends on true Romans, and Rome is
to be found wherever are the true representatives of the city. Yet even this
Lucanian paradox, which dismisses Rome's *maerentia tecta* as ultimately
irrelevant to Roman identity (5.30), draws attention to the deep-rooted
Roman inclination to identify the city precisely with its physical
manifestation.

Rome from Rome?

Eventually the capital of the Roman empire was transferred from Rome.
Strategic considerations had long made the city on the Tiber essentially
marginal to imperial government. Herodian, writing in the early third
century, places a speech in the mouth of one of Commodus' advisers,
dissuading him from neglecting military priorities and hurrying back to
the city, for Rome is wherever the emperor is (1.6.5) – though a speech
made by Severus later in Herodian's history offers a more traditional
perspective (2.10.9). Rome itself was increasingly eclipsed in the third
century. Rome's first Christian emperor, Constantine, planned a new
city, to be named after himself, on the Hellespont.[46] This was to become

---

[45] On the implications of Lucan's use of Camillus, see Masters (1992), 104–6.
[46] Ceausescu (1976), 105–7; Krautheimer (1983), 41–67. Cf. Eusebius *Vita* 3.48. Some
scholars argue that Constantine was not seeking to create a new capital (e.g. Mango
(1985), 34–6), but it is striking that the emperor chose to set up a second senate in
Constantinople.

the capital of the Roman empire (definitively superseding Rome by the early sixth century). Rumours circulated in later years that Constantine himself had transferred the ancient Palladium from Rome to his new city, where it lay buried beneath the porphyry column which bore his statue.

Only an emperor who had embraced a new religion, perhaps, could contemplate abandoning Rome, which continued long afterwards to remain the centre for traditional Roman religious practice, just as it remained the location for the old senate, the chief authority in traditional religious matters.[47] Those senators who remained pagans continued to concern themselves with the traditional religious practices intimately linked with the city of Rome. Symmachus' third *Relatio*, urging the Christian emperor to permit the restoration of the statue of Victory which (until its recent removal) had stood in the senate since the time of Augustus, makes clear the continued perception among pagans of the importance of celebrating traditional cults in their appropriate places. The pagan aristocracy of late antiquity nurtured a sense of religion deeply coloured by reading Livy and Virgil.[48]

Rome later lost its pagan identity to become capital of a new empire, that of the Christian church.[49] But in 1308, almost a thousand years after Constantine's shift of interest to Constantinople, the city was again abandoned, when Pope Clement V moved to Avignon, seeking French protection (the feuds of the nobility had made Rome increasingly dangerous). Some decades later, in the 1370s, the learned Petrarch, seeking to persuade his successor, Pope Urban V, to come back to Rome, turned to celebrations of the city in pagan literature for support.[50] He imagines those who argue that the pope should stay in Avignon invoking Lucan Book 5. If Rome is at Veii, when Camillus is at Veii, so the argument might go, then Rome can be wherever the pope is. Petrarch hesitates to argue against the pope's power to confer significance on wherever he happens to be. Rather he seeks to emphasise the intrinsic superiority of Rome to all other places. For Petrarch the importance of Rome as a place lies in its pagan as much as its Christian history: *quid est enim aliud omnis historia, quam Romana laus?* 'What else is all history if

---

[47] Constantine did build Christian churches in Rome but only outside the monumental centre, which remained the preserve of paganism. Cf. Krautheimer (1983), 25–33.

[48] Cf. Liebeschuetz (1979), 307; Momigliano (1963), 79–99.

[49] Cf. Brown on the Christian appropriation of Roman religious centrality (1967), 289.

[50] *Invectiva contra eum qui maledixit Italiam.*

not the praise of Rome?' Seneca, he says, termed Rome a city *sanctissimam et temperantissimam*. In Petrarch's argument, even pagan perceptions of the religious significance of Rome can have weight.

Rome is somewhat decayed, he admits, but: *non in totum corruit, et quantum graviter imminuta, adhuc tamen est aliquid praeter nomen. muri quidem et palatia ceciderunt: gloria nominis immortalis est*, 'she has not completely fallen and, though gravely damaged, yet she is still something more than a name. Indeed though her palaces and walls have fallen, the glory of her name is immortal.' Petrarch, then, is perhaps readier than the writers of antiquity to dissociate the material city from the city celebrated in literature. Much of his defence of Rome is composed of references to stories of Roman achievement in Livy. The Romans, he argues, are the bravest and greatest of all peoples, hence the continued importance of their city. The religion of those ancient Romans so admired by Petrarch, not surprisingly, receives little explicit attention. Yet, as we saw in the Introduction, Petrarch's attachment to the city as a physical space was especially informed by his intimate knowledge of those early books of Livy's History which had, in antiquity, been central to the construction of Rome's religious identity. It is Livy, whose Camillus set out so persuasively the religious arguments for staying in Rome, whose view of the city most strongly colours Petrarch's conception of its significance. In Petrarch's defence of the city as the true capital of the Christian church, we may perhaps observe a paradoxical sublimation of Livy's celebration of the city as the pre-eminent religious space of traditional Roman paganism.

CHAPTER
3
The city of empire

The moment of conception of Gibbon's *The Decline and Fall of the Roman Empire* (1776–88) is one of the best known of any work of literature: 'It was at Rome, on the fifteenth of October, 1764, as I sat musing amidst the ruins of the Capitol, while the bare-footed fryars were singing Vespers in the temple of Jupiter, that the idea of writing the decline and fall of the city first started to my mind.'[1] Why should inspiration come to Gibbon on the Capitol? This was an area of Rome where, by the mid-eighteenth century, there were few visible remains of antiquity – despite the impression given by Gibbon in this passage. Less erudite visitors to Rome were more often moved to think of its decline amid the spectacular ruins of the Colosseum.[2] Certainly the Capitol, despite being the lowest of Rome's seven hills, afforded extensive views of the rest of the city (though by Gibbon's day it had for several centuries been oriented towards the modern town on the site of the Campus Martius, turning its back on the Roman forum). But Gibbon's choice of location was no doubt primarily determined by the historical significance of the hill. The focal point of the Roman state religion, the Capitol was also seen by ancient Romans as the heart of their empire, the guarantee of its future, the symbol of its aspirations towards eternity. What more suitable viewpoint for the ironic historian of the empire's decline and fall?

The term 'Capitol' is ambiguous, reflecting the ambiguity of *Capitolium*

---

[1] Gibbon (1897), 302.
[2] A tendency which Byron's much-quoted lines from *Childe Harold* IV 141 (1812) and *Manfred* III, IV (1817) were later to encourage. Cf. Mark Twain *The Innocents Abroad* (1869), 252–6.

in ancient Roman usage. Sometimes the latter term designates the southern part of the Capitoline hill in contrast to the northern part, the *arx* – in antiquity the site of the temple of Juno Moneta (these two peaks were separated by a depression where the Asylum was located). Sometimes, particularly in texts of the principate, the term refers to the hill as a whole. And sometimes the term is used to refer to the temple of Jupiter Optimus Maximus, which housed the three deities, Jupiter, Juno and Minerva, known as the Capitoline Triad (and by extension to such temples in other Roman towns).[3] The physical eminence of the hill and the symbolic eminence of the temple are thus often merged in ancient texts. Later the associations of the temple were virtually subsumed by the hill, as the temple itself disappeared, almost without trace.

In antiquity, the Capitol, with its great temple, was one of the most striking sights in Rome, indeed in the world. The first version of the temple of Jupiter Capitolinus, constructed in the sixth century BCE, was decorated with terracotta antefixes in the Etruscan manner, its size unparalleled for centuries to come. When it burnt down in the early first century BCE, its even loftier successor was resplendent with marble and gold.[4] Subsequent temples, rising again from the ashes of disastrous fires, were ever more splendid. The proverbial golden roof of the Temple of Jupiter could be seen gleaming from many parts of the city.[5] References to Rome as the golden city – rich, beautiful and imperishable – can perhaps be read as a metaphorical extension of the goldenness of Rome's chief temple.[6] One aim of this chapter is to explore the various ways in which this one hill and particularly its temple could be made to stand for the city as a whole and even for the entire Roman empire.

The profusion of temples and statues, the rituals associated with the Capitoline hill, asserted its particular role as centre of Roman religion

[3] For examples, see Steinby (1993–), *s.v.*

[4] According to Pliny, the ceiling of the Capitoline temple was gilded as early as 142 BCE, the walls somewhat later. When the temple was rebuilt after the fire of 83 BCE, the roof too received gilding (*NH* 33.57).

[5] On the gold of the Capitol: Virgil *Aen.* 8.348; Ovid *Fasti* 6.73–4; Sen. *Controv.* 1.6.4; 2.1.1; Silius 3.623.

[6] For golden Rome, see Ovid *Ars am.* 3.113; Martial 9.59.2; Auson. *Ordo nob. urb.* 1. Some other temples were also referred to as golden (see e.g. Ovid *Fasti* 1.223–4; *Amores* 3.9.43; Prop. 4.1.5 (all *aurea templa*) and 2.31.1–2 on the Palatine temple of Apollo, constructed under Augustus). On the resonance of the imagery of gold in Augustan literature, see Gros (1976a), 41–2; Feeney (1992), 2; Barker (1993).

and guarantor of empire.[7] The Temple of Jupiter Optimus Maximus stood in a large precinct (the *area Capitolina*) and was decorated with numerous offerings, many of which had been presented by generals after successful military campaigns.[8] The statues and trophies were so many that occasionally space had to be made by removing some.[9] Here was surely the greatest concentration of signs of conquest even in that ultimate city of conquest, Rome.

In the Capitoline temple were kept the archives relating to foreign relations and the Sibylline books (the latter having been placed there by Tarquinius Superbus, according to Livy). Under the republic the senate met here often (and always for the opening meeting of the year), while the *concilium plebis*, the assembly of the plebs, sometimes met here to vote on legislation and judgements. Some of the functions of the Capitoline were later transferred to the Augustan temple of Mars Ultor (while the Sibylline books were transferred to the temple of Apollo Palatinus) but still the Capitol remained the destination for the triumphant Roman general.[10] Clothed in the *tunica palmata* and *toga picta* (the same garments as were worn by the cult statue of Jupiter), his face painted red like that of the statue, the general made his circuitous but glorious way to give thanks to Jupiter Optimus Maximus in front of the Capitoline temple. This ritual of ascent and sacrifice on the Capitoline was the moment when man came closest to god in ancient Rome – no wonder that the Roman imperial family rapidly monopolised the triumph for themselves. But it also had a significance for Rome itself – the moment when it came closest to transcending its impermanent terrestrial form to become the eternal city.

Gibbon's understanding of the significance of the Capitol was based initially at least on his reading of ancient authors (he reminds his readers of his early familiarity with these texts in a footnote to the final chapter of *Decline and Fall*). A consideration of some ways in which the figure of the

---

[7] Among the temples located on the hill were the shrines of Terminus and Iuventas and the temples of Jupiter Feretrius, Jupiter Tonans (built by Augustus), Fides (the divinity invoked as guarantor of treaties), Ops, Veiovis and of course the temple of Juno Moneta on the arx (also the location of the temple of Honour and Virtue built by Marius).

[8] Cf. e.g. Livy 2.22.6, 40.51.3.

[9] For instance on the initiative of the censors in 179 BCE and under Augustus, who had a quantity of statues moved to the Campus Martius (Livy 40.51.3; Suet. *Calig.* 34.1).

[10] On the de-emphasis of the Capitol under Augustus (touched on in Ch. 1 above), see Gros (1976a), 40 and Zanker (1988),108.

Capitol is deployed in Gibbon's writing may draw our attention to the use of this element of Roman topography by some of the ancient authors Gibbon read, in particular Tacitus. Other Roman writers too, not least Livy, explore the association between the Capitoline and Roman imperial power. Both Livy and Tacitus harness the associations of the Capitoline for their own literary and historical ends: in Livy's case a teleological account of the rise of Rome and in Tacitus' an ironic account of its decline (though the ironies and ambiguities of Tacitus' writing are such that the starting-point for any decline remains elusive and the possibilities for progress are never wholly excluded). These two texts contain the most extended discussions of the Capitol in Latin literature. They have undoubtedly had an important influence on subsequent readings of the hill. The latter part of this chapter will consider the subtly shifting symbolic resonance of the Capitoline hill in a number of other ancient literary contexts, before briefly surveying the political role of the Capitol in later Roman history; drastic interventions in the hill's appearance even in this century have been in part prompted by the significance attributed to it in antiquity.

The Capitol in ruins

Scholars have often commented on the artifice with which Gibbon creates his moment of inspiration on the Capitol (there are three different versions extant, as well as a similar comment at the end of *Decline and Fall* itself).[11] Appropriately for a contemplation of decline, the season is autumn, the time of day, as indicated by the singing of Vespers, late. The myth of origin Gibbon offers, as Patricia Craddock observes, 'emphasises the ironic complexity of the "ruins" that inspired him'.[12] The friars are described as singing, not in their church, that of Santa Maria in Aracoeli, but rather in the temple of Jupiter Optimus Maximus, which Gibbon believed (following scholarly authorities such as Nardini) to have been located on the same site.[13]

---

[11] Discussed by Craddock (1984), 63–82. For literary influences on Gibbon's account see New (1978).

[12] Craddock (1984), 64.

[13] This higher part of the Capitol, as noted above, is now generally agreed to have been the location of the temple of Juno Moneta, the temple of Jupiter being sited rather on the part of the hill nearer the river. For Gibbon's view of Capitoline topography, see (1909–14), VII 235–6 with note 47. Cf. Nardini (1666), 296–309.

Though another building has taken its place, for Gibbon the Temple of Jupiter is still present. For the educated (though in this case mistaken) eye of the historian, place activates memory, calling up earlier traces in the urban palimpsest.[14] Conducting their rites in the temple, the monks appear as an intrusion into the traditional pagan sanctity of the Capitol; there is an implicit suggestion that they have some responsibility for the decline of the Roman empire. At the same time, the ironic mode of Gibbon's history is, as Stephen Bann points out, established in this juxtaposition of great pagan temple and lowly Christian friars.[15]

It is not only the Temple of Jupiter whose presence depends on Gibbon's erudite imagination. The ruins too among which the historian sits were by Gibbon's day present only through memory. In the journal written during his visit to Rome in 1764, Gibbon remarks on the grandeur of the modern Capitol, where Michelangelo's square was surrounded on three sides by buildings whose architecture was not entirely to Gibbon's taste but which could scarcely be described as ruined.[16] Craddock terms Gibbon's ruins metaphorical and indeed they can be seen as functioning metaphorically in his view of Rome. They can also be seen as a historical and literary presence, recalling earlier viewers of Rome, as the last chapter of *Decline and Fall* itself reveals.

Having, in the second half of *Decline and Fall*, surveyed the history of the eastern empire, from the fall of Rome to the fall of Constantinople, Gibbon moves back in the last three chapters of his history to the ancient centre of the empire, the place from which he began, the city of Rome. In the last chapter of all, he takes his readers to Rome's metonymic heart, the Capitoline hill – but not the hill in Gibbon's own time. We visit the Capitol with a fifteenth-century scholar and member of the papal curia Poggio Bracciolini, whose treatise *De varietate fortunae* was composed in the 1430s and 1440s, around the time of the fall of Constantinople. The first half of Poggio's first book, part of which is translated and paraphrased by Gibbon, consists of a dialogue on the ruins of Rome: 'The place and the object gave ample scope for moralising on the vicissitudes of fortune, which spares neither man nor the proudest of his works, which buries empires and cities in a common grave.'[17] In Poggio's day the ruins on the Capitol were a material presence.

[14] Cf. Ernst (forthcoming).
[15] Bann (forthcoming).
[16] Gibbon (1961), 239.
[17] Gibbon (1909–14), VII 313. For the Latin text, see Poggio Bracciolini (1993).

Gibbon also quotes Poggio's reference to Virgil's description of the pre-Roman Capitol in *Aeneid* 8: 'This Tarpeian rock was then a savage and solitary thicket: in the time of the poet, it was crowned with the golden roofs of a temple: the temple is overthrown, the gold has been pillaged, the wheel of fortune has accomplished her revolution and the sacred ground is again disfigured with thorns and brambles.' In ceding the opening of his last chapter to Poggio, Gibbon includes in his own narrative the traditional ruin-inspired musings on fortune's vicissitudes, while at the same time distancing himself from them.[18] Gibbon does not here surrender himself to humanist nostalgia for Rome; as O'Brien points out: 'Gibbon comes to bury Rome not to praise it.'[19]

Chapter 69 of Gibbon's history, by contrast (the first of the final three chapters), referring back to the establishment of the Roman Comune in the twelfth century, presents us with a Capitol newly reincorporated into Roman civic life. 'It was the first act of the Romans, an act of freedom, to restore the strength, though not the beauty of the Capitol; to fortify the seat of their arms and counsels; and as often as they ascended the hill, the coldest minds must have glowed with the remembrance of their ancestors.'[20] We might remember that, though Gibbon himself claimed to have a 'temper . . . not very susceptible of enthusiasm', the remains of Rome had the power to set even that cool ironist alight, when he at last came to the eternal city.[21] Gibbon presents the Capitoline hill as offering particular inspiration to latter-day Romans; it is this hill which embodies the memory of pre-papal Roman power.

The Capitol in flames

The passage on the later development of the Capitol in Chapter 69 comes at the end of a short account of the history of the hill, the early part of which is largely based on two chapters in the *Histories* of Tacitus (3.71–2). Tacitus was the ancient historian Gibbon admired most.[22] The

---

[18] On the tradition of ruin-writing, see Introduction, above.
[19] I am grateful to Karen O'Brien for allowing me to read her essay in advance of publication.
[20] Gibbon (1909–14), VII 236. This development will be discussed further below.
[21] Gibbon (1897), 267.
[22] Cf. Cartledge (1989); Womersley (1988), 80–8; Jordan (1971), 174–83.

ends to which he deploys Tacitus' ironic treatment of the Capitol add a new dimension to the complex literary resonance of this particular feature of Roman topography.

The physical fabric of the city of Rome generally plays little part in Tacitus' writings. His last work, the *Annals*, though it begins with the words *urbem Romam*, makes few references to the material city. When, for instance, the state of the empire on the death of Augustus is described, only the briefest reference is made to that emperor's thorough-going transformation of the city's appearance: those who regarded the Augustan regime favourably spoke of *urbem ipsam magnifico ornatu*, 'the magnificent adornment of the city itself', reports Tacitus (1.9).[23] This reticence on the subject of the city in the *Annals* retrospectively heightens the significance of the city's role in the *Histories*, Tacitus' account of the civil conflict of 69 CE, the 'year of the four emperors', through to the reign of Domitian (only the first few books survive), where the city's presence is far more prominent.[24]

In the *Histories*, repeated mention of the city's buildings serves as a reminder that this text is concerned with civil wars, some of whose battles are fought in the very streets of the empire's capital. A sharp distinction was traditionally drawn between places outside the city, where Romans might bear arms, and the space within the city (that is within the *pomerium*) where armed Romans were only allowed with special permission. When citizens met in military groupings, even if only for the purposes of voting, they met in the Campus Martius, the field of Mars, god of war, which lay outside the *pomerium* (Mars had no temple within the *pomerium* before the construction of the temple of Mars Ultor under Augustus). A successful general and his army would wait in the Campus Martius until the senate granted them permission for a triumph. Only then could they undertake a triumphal procession, leading around the Velia, down the sacred way, through the forum and up to the Capitol, culminating at the temple of Jupiter Capitolinus.[25] That ceremonial breaching of the civil/military spatial distinction was an exception to normal practice, which marked the *triumphator* as himself exceptional.

---

[23] *Ann.* 15.43 (discussed briefly in Ch. 2 above) treats Nero's rebuilding of the city after the fire of 64. References to monuments in Tacitus are collected and analysed by Rouveret (1991). She emphasises their rarity.

[24] On the city in *Hist.* see Rouveret (1991), 3069–72.

[25] For details see Coarelli (1968) and Nicolet (1980), 352–6.

While the distinction came to be compromised under the principate, as
the praetorian guard became a visible presence in the city, something of
its symbolic significance nevertheless remained. I shall consider the role
of the city generally as battlefield in Tacitus' *Histories* before focusing
more specifically on his treatment of the Capitol.

In Tacitus' *Histories*, the aged emperor Galba, Nero's successor, meets
his end at the hands of Roman soldiers in the Roman forum:

> agebatur huc illuc Galba vario turbae fluctuantis impulsu, completis
> undique basilicis ac templis, lugubri prospectu. neque populi aut
> plebis ulla vox, sed attoniti vultus et conversae ad omnia aures; non
> tumultus, non quies, quale magni metus et magnae irae silentium est.
> Othoni tamen armari plebem nuntiabatur; ire praecipitis et occupare
> pericula iubet. igitur milites Romani, quasi Vologaesum aut Pacorum
> avito Arsacidarum solio depulsuri ac non imperatorem suum inermem
> et senem trucidare pergerent, disiecta plebe, proculcato senatu, truces
> armis, rapidi equis forum inrumpunt. nec illos Capitolii aspectus et
> imminentium templorum religio et priores et futuri principes terruere
> quo minus facerent scelus cuius ultor est quisquis successit.

> Galba was being carried hither and thither by the wavering pressure of
> the turbulent crowd. On every side the basilicas and temples were
> packed, a wretched sight. No word was spoken by the populace; their
> faces were tense, their ears alert to every sound. No clamour, no peace
> either, only the silence of great fear and great anger. However, Otho,
> told that the people were taking arms, ordered his men to rush in and
> forestall the danger. And so Roman soldiers, as if bent on unseating
> from the ancestral throne of the Arsacids Vologaeses or Pacorus, set
> out to slaughter the unarmed old man who was their own emperor.
> Scattering the people, trampling the senate, armed to the teeth, their
> horses galloping, they burst into the Forum. Nor were they frightened
> by the sight of the Capitol and the religious power of the temples
> looming over them, nor the thought of emperors past and emperors to
> come – for the crime they were committing would be avenged by the
> victim's successor, whoever he might be.   (*Hist.* 1.40)

Tacitus' description moves vividly from horrified quiet to the terror
created by the Roman army – in a parody of the heroic campaigns of old
– galloping into the Roman forum to murder the emperor. The

monuments of the city – above all those of the Capitol – personify Roman history, as the last sentence juxtaposes the buildings looking down on the forum with the thought of past emperors (whose statues would, of course, have been a ubiquitous presence in this part of the city) and emperors to come. Even for Tacitus the overwhelming majesty of the physical aspect of Rome is hard to resist, though it is undercut by the final twist: self-interest at least should have dissuaded the supporters of Otho from slaying Galba (and indeed Tacitus reports at 1.44 that Vitellius, the next emperor but one, later dealt with those who claimed responsibility).

As the army approaches, civilians evacuate the forum. In the panic, Galba is thrown from his chair. Tacitus locates this at a specific place in the forum *iuxta Curtii lacum*, beside the *lacus Curtius* (1.41). It is here that the emperor is killed, dying heroically or perhaps not (Tacitus is characteristically open-minded) – a plurality of possibilities which might be seen as reflecting the several versions of the legend associated with the *lacus*, some presenting Curtius as a Roman hero, others as Sabine enemy.[26] The site of Galba's death later had a notoriety attractive to visitors, Tacitus writes – at least to the uncouth barbarians who came to Rome as Vitellius' soldiers (2.88).

The death of Galba's supporter Titus Vinius is also reported with topographical precision – *ante aedem divi Iulii* , 'in front of the temple of the deified Julius Caesar' (1.42) – a reminder that killing the ruler in the heart of the city is an old Roman tradition. Piso, Galba's chosen successor, manages to escape immediate death, thanks to the centurion Sempronius Densus, who sacrifices himself to provide cover. Piso takes refuge in the Temple of Vesta and, with the help of the temple slave, evades his pursuers. Tacitus is quick to point out that he was protected not by the sanctity of the temple and its rituals but only by escaping notice – *non religione nec caerimoniis sed latebra* (1.43). The precariousness of such protection is soon revealed, for his end is only briefly deferred. Two of Otho's soldiers, oblivious of the sacred location, drag him out and murder him on the temple steps – *in foribus templi*. The incestuous pollution of civil war infects Roman religion and Roman history, embodied in particular sacred places, named one by one, around the forum.

---

[26] See end of Ch.1 above.

The city next appears as a scene of conflict near the end of Book I,
when owing to a misunderstanding (a frequent motive force in Tacitus'
account), some soldiers arm themselves and surround Otho, the new
emperor, in his palace (1.80–5). The troops are eventually persuaded to
return to their barracks but such fear has been aroused that the following
day Rome resembles a captured city, the houses closed up, few people in
the street, the populace miserable – *velut capta urbe clausae domus, rarus
per vias populus, maesta plebs* (1.82).[27] This incident, not in itself of great
significance, foreshadows the disaster which will afflict the city at a later
stage in the conflict.

The city's most spectacular appearance in the *Histories* comes in the
prelude to the decisive establishment of Flavian ascendancy. Battle rages
in the centre of Rome, while the crowds look on as though at the games,
cheering first one side then the other:

> saeva ac deformis urbe tota facies: alibi proelia et vulnera, alibi
> balneae popinaeque; simul cruor et strues corporum, iuxta scorta et
> scortis similes; quantum in luxurioso otio libidinum, quidquid in
> acerbissima captivitate scelerum, prorsus ut eandem civitatem et
> furere crederes et lascivire. conflixerant et ante armati exercitus in
> urbe, bis Lucio Sulla, semel Cinna victoribus, nec tunc minus
> crudelitatis: nunc inhumana securitas et ne minimo quidem temporis
> voluptates intermissae: velut festis diebus id quoque gaudium accederet,
> exultabant, fruebantur, nulla partium cura, malis publicis laeti.

> Everything in the city bore a savage and perverted aspect. On the one
> hand battles and wounds, on the other baths and taverns; together
> blood and heaps of corpses next to prostitutes and those no better
> than prostitutes. The excesses of pleasure associated with luxurious
> peace were intermingled with the excesses of crime accompanying the
> most savage sack. You would think the city raved with madness and
> sensuality at one and the same time. Earlier, too, armies with their
> weapons had clashed in Rome, twice with Lucius Sulla the victor,
> once with Cinna – nor was there any less cruelty on those occasions.
> But now there was a brutal indifference and not the slightest moment

---

[27] Bloodier characteristics of the *urbs capta* are attributed to Rome in the aftermath of
Vitellius' defeat at 4.1. For a discussion of Tacitus' treatment of civil war, see Keitel
(1984), 306–25 (309–10 on *Hist.*).

of respite from pleasures. A kind of holiday enjoyment prevailed, the people were thrilled and had their fun, heedless of the two sides, happy amid public misfortune. (*Hist.* 3.83)

This is ironic history with a vengeance. In Tacitus' hands, civil war, that most traditional of Roman subjects, acquires a novel horror. Romans fight in the heart of the city – that had been done before, Tacitus points out. This time there is a satiric twist. The onlookers have been so corrupted that they can no longer apprehend the horror (one might contrast this with the fighting described in Book 1, when, anticipating the attack on Galba in the forum, the people were terrified, and when, after the mutiny suppressed by Otho, the plebs was *maesta*, 1.40 and 1.82). The only terms now in which the carnage can make sense to Romans are those of their entertainments.

In Tacitus' narrative, the destruction of the Capitol by fire in 69 CE takes on a particular charge. Fighting within the city is an appalling transgression of traditional category distinctions; fighting on the Capitol is a suicidal assault on the central symbol of Roman imperial power and Roman religion. He comments in his preface on the dreadful fate of Italy during the civil wars: *et urbs incendiis vastata, consumptis antiquissimis delubris, ipso Capitolio civium manibus incenso,* 'the city was devastated by fires, the most ancient shrines were destroyed and the Capitol itself was fired by the hands of Roman citizens' (1.2). The destruction of the Capitol, in the course of fighting between the supporters of Vitellius and the Flavian party (whose candidate Vespasian would eventually be successful) is described in Book 3. Vitellius claims to have abdicated but retains control of the palace; Sabinus, the leading Flavian, takes control of the Capitol. No longer heeding their commanders, the sometime supporters of Vitellius attack the Capitoline. The defenders use the tiles and stones of the porticos of the *clivus Capitolinus* as missiles, then uproot the statues, *decora maiorum*, to serve as a barricade. The Vitellians attack in two directions from the Asylum and from the Hundred Steps by the Tarpeian rock. Whether the Flavians started the fire in self-defence or whether the Vitellians were thereby attempting to force them to surrender is left open. But the temple itself catches fire and is destroyed:

id facinus post conditam urbem luctuosissimum foedissimumque rei publicae populi Romani accidit, nullo externo hoste, propitiis, si per

mores nostros licet, deis, sedem Iovis Optimi Maximi auspicato a
maioribus pignus imperii conditam, quam non Porsenna dedita urbe
neque Galli capta temerare potuissent, furore principum excindi.

This evil deed was, since the foundation of the city, the most grievous
and foul to have befallen the republic of the people of Rome. Without
external enemies, the gods (if our conduct permitted) well disposed,
the temple of Jupiter Best and Greatest, inaugurated by our ancestors
and founded as the guarantee of our empire, the temple which neither
Porsenna, after the city's surrender, not the Gauls after its capture
dared to touch, was burnt down by the madness of Roman leaders.

(Hist. 3.72)

The emperor Otho had earlier assured his troops that the essence of the
city lay in its people, above all the senators, and not in its buildings, which
muta ista et inanima intercidere ac reparari promisca sunt, 'are voiceless
and without spirit; it does not matter if they are destroyed or rebuilt'
(1.84). But for Tacitus the destruction of this one building outweighs
every other disaster that has ever befallen the city. The temple of Jupiter
is the *pignus imperii* – the guarantee of Roman empire – but it is the
Romans themselves, always their own worst enemies, but never more so
than now, who have destroyed it. What is significant is not so much the
loss of the building itself, which has indeed been destroyed and rebuilt
before, but the manner of its destruction.

A brief digression then tells us the history of the Capitol. The reference
to specific places on the Capitoline hill in the previous chapter (71), the
clivus Capitolinus, the Asylum, the Tarpeian rock, will perhaps have
already put the reader in mind of the earliest age of Roman history, as
recounted by Livy (to be discussed further below), whose History *ab urbe
condita* is also evoked by the phrase *post conditam urbem.* Livy's uplifting
account of Rome's rise from humble beginnings is thus appropriated to
give an added edge to Tacitus' indictment of his compatriots' capacity for
self-destruction.

Tacitus' account of the history of the temple encapsulates the history
of the entire city. The temple was originally vowed by the elder Tarquin,
the scale of the foundations he laid reflecting hopes for Rome's future
rather than its current position. Though building continued under
subsequent kings, the temple was only completed under the free republic.
Burnt down in 83 BCE, it was rebuilt by Sulla. As the dictator did not live

to complete it, the temple was dedicated by the consul Lutatius Catulus. Tacitus concludes by noting that the inscription recording his name survived among all the great works of Rome's emperors until the civil wars of 69. Thus the temple, though built under Rome's kings and rebuilt under a dictator, had none-the-less been dedicated by the magistrates of the free republic on both occasions. Catulus' name had remained, a reminder of the days when other names besides that of Caesar might stand on the greatest of Rome's public buildings.

The Capitol had also been restored by Augustus, after it was hit by a thunderbolt in 9 BCE. Tacitus does not mention this episode, which was perhaps not very convenient for his narrative. Even the Augustan temple bore the name of Catulus, however. Augustus boasted in his *Res gestae* that when he restored the Capitol he deliberately omitted to inscribe his own name on it (20.1). The Capitol of Tacitus' own day revealed a lack of Augustan restraint on the part of its author. Domitian, Suetonius records, when he restored the Capitol after the fire of 80 CE, inscribed only his own name, omitting those of all previous builders: *omnia sub titulo suo ac sine ulla pristini auctoris memoria* (*Dom.* 5).[28]

Gibbon's use of the city, echoing that of Tacitus, evokes also Tacitus' reflections on the Roman capacity for self-destruction. In Gibbon's account of the causes of the ruin into which the city has fallen (Ch. 71), by far the largest portion of blame is attributed to the Romans themselves. 'Our fancy may create, or adopt, a pleasing romance, that the Goths and Vandals sallied forth from Scandinavia, ardent to avenge the flight of Odin, to break the chains and to chastise the oppressors of mankind; that they wished to burn the records of classic literature and to found their national architecture on the broken members of the Tuscan and Corinthian orders. But in simple truth, the northern conquerors were neither sufficiently savage nor sufficiently refined to entertain such aspiring ideas of destruction and revenge.'[29] Rather 'the last and most potent and forcible cause of destruction' was for Gibbon, 'the domestic hostilities of the Romans themselves'.[30]

The Capitoline temple is the symbol of Roman empire, the *pignus imperii*, in Tacitus' words – an association which, as we shall see from

---

[28] On Domitian's temple, see also Plut. *Publ.* 15.3–5, though Plutarch asserts that its magnificence is outdone by that of Domitian's palace.

[29] Gibbon (1909–14), VII 321.

[30] *Ibid.*, 326.

earlier literature, was well established. The Capitol is the obvious vantage point from which to survey both city and empire. This is the place where Gibbon claims to have conceived his history and from which he speaks in drawing the history to a close. Tacitus' account of the temple's destruction, however, suggests a more ironic significance for Gibbon's choice of this part of Rome. The Capitoline hill in Tacitus' account of the civil war becomes the place where the Roman capacity for self-destruction reaches its culmination – unmissably spectacular and irretrievably devastating (though the temple is rebuilt under Vespasian (4.53), the scars of civil war can never be fully healed). In evoking this particular literary precedent in Chapter 69, Gibbon sets the scene for his own account of later Roman self-destruction in the last chapter of his history.

Head of empire

I suggested above that some elements in Tacitus' account of the history and destruction of the Capitoline might be read as evoking Livy's version of the earliest years of Rome's history and, in particular, of the origins of a number of topographical features in the city. Livy's first five books, unlike the other extant parts of his history, pay considerable attention to the topography of Rome. Events associated with the mythical and distant days of regal Rome could seem vividly present to readers many centuries later, for they are shown taking place in the physical space, among the topographical features, familiar to inhabitants of the city in Augustus' time. Livy, mentioning the place where Romulus and Remus were found, comments, *vastae tum in his locis solitudines erant*, 'At that time, these places were wild and deserted' (1.4.6). The site of Rome is inhabited only by wolves and shepherds. Yet Livy does not generally lay much emphasis on the physical contrast between Romulean and Augustan Rome. Though his history opens with a nostalgic reference to the never-to-be-recaptured virtue of the Roman past (1.pr.5), the Roman landscape is generally used to establish similarity and continuity rather than difference or rupture (one might contrast the use made of Rome's physical fabric by some of Livy's contemporaries, discussed in Chapter 1 above). His aetiological treatment of elements of the city (no doubt much influenced by Varro) serves to establish an intimate connection between the early history of the Roman state, its future destiny as an imperial power and its physical form.

Features of Rome's landscape first appear in Chapter 4 of Book 1, when Romulus and Remus are exposed as infants beside the *ficus Ruminalis*. In subsequent chapters of this book regal Rome is evoked place by place: the Palatine (which even then hosted the Lupercalia) fortified by Romulus, the Asylum on the Capitol, the temple of Jupiter Feretrius (also on the Capitol, the first temple dedicated at Rome), the *lacus Curtius*, the *palus Capreae*, the temple of Janus, the grove of Egeria, the Caelian Hill, the Curia Hostilia, the Pons Sublicius (Rome's first bridge), the prison, the Circus Maximus.

The Capitol receives extensive treatment. Even under Romulus it is associated with military success. It was on this hill, Livy records, that Romulus dedicated the spoils won in his war against the Caecinenses and their king Acron (1.10.5). Alongside the sacred oak where he made his dedication, Romulus marked out the plan of the temple of Jupiter Feretrius, instructing that within its sacred precinct Roman commanders would in future dedicate the spoils of honour (*spolia opima*) when they had killed kings and commanders of the enemy. Already, Jupiter and the Capitol are associated with Roman victories.

After successes in war against the Sabines and others, Rome's fifth king, Tarquinius Priscus, embarks on a number of projects in the city. The completion of a city wall is resumed and Tarquin also sets about draining low-lying parts of the city by means of sewers, *et aream ad aedem in Capitolio Iovis, quam voverat bello Sabino, iam praesagiente animo futuram olim amplitudinem loci occupat fundamentis*, 'and, foreseeing the splendour the place would one day have, he laid foundations for the temple of Jupiter on the Capitol, which he had vowed in the Sabine war' (1.38.7).[31] The phrase *futuram . . . amplitudinem* refers most obviously to the temple's enormous size, even in its earliest manifestation; it can also be read as applying to Rome in general (indeed this is how Tacitus interprets the passage at *Hist.* 3.71, discussed above). The physical form of the city is presented in Livy's narrative as an index of Roman power. Romulus expands the city in anticipation of increased power and population (1.8). Later extensions to the territory ruled by Rome are mirrored in extensions to the city (1.44).[32] The Capitol and Jupiter already have a role here; Livy records that the Romulean temple of Jupiter Feretrius was enlarged as a

[31] For the association of sewers with the Etruscan kings of Rome see Ch. 4 below.
[32] Cf. Tac. *Ann.* 12.23–4 on later expansion of the *pomerium*. On the development of the *pomerium*, see Coarelli (1983), 262–4.

response to military successes (1.33). Even before the Capitoline temple is
built, there is in Livy's narrative a significant relation between Jupiter, the
Capitol and the territorial extent of Roman dominion.

The temple begun by Tarquinius Priscus is largely constructed under
his son, Rome's last king, Tarquinius Superbus, who wants to use the
plunder from his victory over the Volsci to ensure *eam amplitudinem Iovis
templi quae digna deum hominumque rege, quae Romano imperio, quae
ipsius etiam loci maiestate esset*, 'a temple of Jupiter so splendid that it
would be worthy of the king of gods and men, worthy of the Roman
empire, and worthy of the majesty of the place itself' (1.53.3). The
relation between temple and empire is here made more explicit. After
further military successes, Tarquin again turns his attention to the city.
Livy gives an extensive description of the preparations for construction
of the Capitoline temple. Tarquin decides, so that the site may be entirely
dedicated to Jupiter, to clear away other shrines: *inter principia condendi
huius operis movisse numen ad indicandam tanti imperii molem traditur
deos*, 'Just as the work was beginning, tradition says the gods signified
their will to show the greatness of the mighty empire' (1.55.3). The
auguries permit the removal of all shrines but that of the god Terminus.[33]
The immovability of Terminus is taken as a sign that Roman power will
be immovable (paradoxically, given that the success of the ever-expanding
empire requires the frequent displacement of its boundaries).

Livy records that, after this auspice of permanence had been received,
another prodigy followed, also portending the greatness of the empire:

> caput humanum integra facie aperientibus fundamenta templi dicitur
> apparuisse. quae visa species haud per ambages arcem eam imperii
> caputque rerum fore portendebat; idque ita cecinere vates, quique in
> urbe erant quosque ad eam rem consultandam ex Etruria acciverant.
>
> A human head, its face intact, is said to have appeared to those who
> were digging the foundations of the temple. This manifestation clearly
> revealed that this place was to be citadel of the empire and the capital
> of the world. Such was the prediction of the seers, both those within
> the city and those who had been summoned from Etruria to give
> advice in the matter.   (1.55.5–6)

---

[33] At 5.54.7 Livy makes Camillus claim that the shrine of Iuventas also remained in the
area Capitolina to be incorporated in the new temple.

This aetiological myth (similar versions appear in Varro, Dionysius of Halicarnassus and elsewhere) is heavy with significance.[34] Romans associated the head, *caput*, with height, with origins and with power.[35] The Capitoline, rising above the city, is the context for a collection of originary myths and the seat of power of Rome's chief deity, Jupiter Optimus Maximus, the most sacred place in Rome. The story explains the name of the hill, at the same time offering historical legitimation for Rome's imperial project. Earlier, Livy described how Romulus, in his last words before his apotheosis (according to the report of Proculus Iulius), told of the will of heaven that Rome be *caput orbis terrarum* (1.16.7). The leaders of the Latins were, in the time of Servius Tullius, obliged to concede that Rome was *caput rerum* (1.45.3), he records. The portent of the human head actualises and confirms this metaphor.

An acropolis or citadel, such as the Roman Capitol, was a characteristic feature of Greek cities, and those modelled on them, of the sixth century BCE. But later Romans saw their city as, even in those early days, more than just another city-state. Versions of the portent of the head have parallels in stories associated with the foundation of Carthage, Rome's great rival imperial power.[36] The Capitol was the seat not of day-to-day political power in Rome (most meetings of the senate and of the people took place elsewhere), but rather of Rome's symbolic power.[37]

Livy's description of the early history of the Capitol was in part a response to the architectural and ritual connections between this particular part of Rome and conceptions of Rome's imperial power in the late republic and principate. His narrative, hugely influential for later Romans' conceptions of Rome, also served to reinforce the symbolic associations of this part of the city. The history of the Capitol is presented by Livy as making the Roman empire inevitable; the Capitol becomes the ideological sign of Roman imperialism.

[34] Varro *Ling.* 5.41; Dion. Hal. 4.59.1–61.2.
[35] Cf. Bourgeaud (1987), 86–100.
[36] Bourgeaud (1987), 98–100. See also Ogilvie (1970), *ad loc.* These parallels reinforce Bourgeaud's argument that this complex of myths probably did not grow up until the fourth or third centuries, when Rome's imperial aspirations really took off (1987), 91–2.
[37] Borgeaud (1987), 91.

Urbs aeterna

The ritual of the triumph, culminating on the Capitol, celebrated the acquisition of new territories for the Roman empire and the successful defence of those already held. It was from the Capitol that Rome looked out over its possessions. Ovid, describing the rites on the Capitol to mark the taking of office by the first consuls of the year, concludes:

> Iuppiter arce sua totum cum spectat in orbem,
>   nil nisi Romanum, quod tueatur, habet.

> Jupiter, as he surveys the world from his citadel, sees nothing
> that is not Roman.   *(Fasti* 1.85–6)

It was Jupiter who received thanks for the past successes of the empire and who guaranteed Rome's imperial future. In Virgil's *Aeneid* (1.279), like Livy's history, a teleological justification for Roman imperialism, Jupiter is made to promise the Romans *imperium sine fine* – an empire without bounds spatial or temporal.

The Capitol also symbolised the invincibility of Rome, for it was believed that only this part of the city had never been occupied by a foreign enemy; the attacks even of Lars Porsenna and of the Gauls had left the heart of Rome unscathed (a belief which made even more horrific the Romans' own destruction of this part of the city during the civil war of 69 CE).[38] Conversely the enemies of Rome are regularly presented as setting their sights specifically on control of the Capitol. Horace describes celebrations as premature while: *Capitolio | regina dementis ruinas | funus et imperio parabat*, 'the frenzied queen prepared ruin for the Capitol and death to the empire' *(Carm.* 1.37.6–8).[39] Similarly Silius Italicus, in his epic account of the Punic wars, describes the soldiers of Hannibal eager to possess the Capitol.[40]

The fate of Rome itself was perceived as in a sense dependent on the Capitol's fate. Tacitus tells of rebellious Gauls in 69 CE spurred on to defy Rome, when they hear the Capitol has burnt, for they take this to

---

[38] Not all ancient writers concur here. Skutsch discusses the tradition that the Gauls did occupy the Capitol (1968), 138–42.

[39] Similarly Cleopatra, for Ovid's Jupiter, vainly threatened that 'our Capitol would yield to her Canopus', *servitura suo Capitolia nostra Canopo (Met.* 15.828).

[40] Sil. 4.150–1, 7.492–3, 9.544–6. The Capitol is of particular significance in Silius' epic where Hannibal's threat to Rome is to be repulsed by Jupiter's intervention.

mean the end of the Roman empire (*Hist.* 4.54.2) – no doubt a projection of Roman anxieties. In the fourth century, Ammianus Marcellinus, describing the Temple of Serapis in Alexandria, draws a comparison with the Capitol in Rome: *atriis . . . columnatis amplissimis, et spirantibus signorum figmentis, et reliqua operum multitudine ita est exornatum, ut post Capitolium, quo se venerabilis Roma in aeternum attollit, nihil orbis terrarum ambitiosius cernat*, 'so splendid with its most spacious columned halls, with its statues that almost seem to breathe and a multitude of other works of art, that, after the Capitol, with which venerable Rome elevates itself to eternity, the world sees nothing more impressive' (22.16.12).[41] In the much quoted aphorism, wrongly attributed to the Venerable Bede (and best known in Byron's translation), the Colosseum is the guarantee of Rome's durability, while Rome itself guarantees that of the world.[42] But for the Romans of antiquity it was the great golden temple of Jupiter, overlooking the forum, which guaranteed the future of their city and their world. If Rome can function as a metonymy of the world (as frequent plays on *urbs* and *orbis*, discussed in Chapter 4 below, imply), then the Capitol functions as a metonymy of Rome itself. Ammianus makes clear the Capitol's significance as the place where Rome strives to transcend history.

References to Rome's eternity (often explicitly associated with the Capitol) appear to begin in the Augustan period; the phrase *urbs aeterna* first occurs in Tibullus.[43] The idea is, however, foreshadowed in Cicero's speech of 63 BCE, *Pro Gaio Rabirio*, where, defending his client's involvement in the killing of the alleged demagogue Saturninus, Cicero argues that men of violence within the Roman state are, now that all foreign enemies have been vanquished, the only threat to the eternity of the Roman empire (33). By implication such threats had been eradicated with the establishment of the Augustan regime, when several writers refer without qualification to the eternity of the city.

The association of the Capitol with Rome's eternity could be made to serve poetic purposes too. Roman writers of this period in particular use

---

[41] On Ammianus' idea of the eternity of Rome, see Matthews (1986). The historian's usual term for the city is *urbs aeterna*.

[42] Cf. Purcell (1992), 427.

[43] See Hardie (1992), 61 and Mellor (1981), 1018–25 . Similar phrases occur in Livy (4.4.4; 5.7.10; 28.28.11). Cf. Miles (1986).

the Capitol as a guarantee of the future of their own work. Virgil apostrophises on the deaths of Nisus and Euryalus:

> fortunati ambo! si quid mea carmina possunt
> nulla dies umquam memori vos eximet aevo,
> dum domus Aeneae Capitoli immobile saxum
> accolet imperiumque pater Romanus habebit.

> O fortunate pair! If my poetry has any power, never will you fade from the memory of the age, so long as the house of Aeneas occupies the Capitol's unyielding rock and the Roman father holds the empire.   (*Aeneid* 9.446–9)

Horace also ties the fate of his poetry to the fate of the Capitol. The concluding poem of the third book of Odes presents his work as more durable than bronze and more lofty than the pyramids of the Pharaohs, a claim which has been read as asserting the superiority of the written monument to the built monument (and hence of Horace's work to that of Augustus).[44] Yet the poem continues:

> ...usque ego postera
> crescam laude recens, dum Capitolium
> scandet cum tacita virgine pontifex.

> I shall continue to grow with fresh praise, so long as the pontifex, together with the silent vestal, climbs the Capitol.   (*Carm.* 3.30.7–9)

While the poem may outlive specific monuments yet its survival is presented as dependent on Rome, as symbolised by this particular part of the city's topography. The durability of the Capitol for Horace relates not so much to the buildings on the hill as to the perpetuation of the religious rites which are an intrinsic part of what the Capitol and of what Rome signifies.[45] Statius later uses the durability of the Capitol (newly restored by Domitian) as a promise of the future of Roman festivals (*Silvae* 1.6.98–102). The future of Rome – of Latin *mores,* religion and literature – is assured by the Capitol's existence.

[44] See Jaeger (1990), 141.
[45] Ovid makes a similar claim for his poetry, tying its future to Rome's continuing empire rather than to the Capitol itself (*Tristia* 3.7.47–52), though elsewhere Ovid may be found hinting at the transience of Rome. On this see Hardie (1992), 60–1.

Decapitation

How were perceptions of the Capitol affected when Rome's continued existence seemed less secure? Jerome, lamenting the sack of Rome in 410, writes *Romani imperii truncatum caput! et ut verius dicam, in una urbe totus orbis interiit,* 'the head of the Roman empire was cut off, and, to speak more truly, the entire world perished with that single city' (*Commentary to Ezekiel* pr.).[46] Drawing on the verbal resemblance of *urbs* and *orbis*, Jerome here presents the world as destroyed along with the destruction of the city. He does not explicitly mention the Capitol. Yet in speaking of the beheading of the Roman empire Jerome evokes the same image of head and body which Roman writers used to explain the name of the Capitoline hill. The power of Jerome's lament comes not only from the imagery of beheading but also from the invocation of the traditional symbol of Rome's eternity at the very moment when the empire seems destroyed.

The golden temple of Jupiter did not long outlast the Roman empire. In the mid fifth century, for instance, Gaiseric, according to Procopius, removed a large portion of the roof during the Vandal wars (*Vandal Wars* 3.5.4) – though the temple is still described as one of the wonders of the world by Cassiodorus (*Variae* 7.6) in the early years of the sixth century (part of a list which may be tralatitious).[47] Isidorus in the seventh century speaks of the Capitol in the past tense: *Capitolium Romae vocatum eo quod fuerit Romanae urbis et religionis caput summum,* 'The Capitol at Rome was so called because it was summit and source of the Roman city and religion' (*Etym.* 15.2.31). Yet the symbolic associations of the hill persisted; the Capitol, covered in ruins, largely occupied by monks, and sometimes referred to as Monte Caprino – the Hill of the Goats – continued to represent the imperial might of pagan Rome.[48] An ancient legend, recounted by Magister Gregorius (writing probably in the twelfth century), told of a multitude of statues on the ancient Capitol, each representing a race or region of the Roman empire (*Mirabilia* 8). If any people rebelled against Roman government, a silver bell would ring on

---

[46] On the complexities of Jerome's attitude to Rome, see Paschoud (1967), 209–21.

[47] On the destruction of the temple of Jupiter, see Lanciani (1902), 1.58.

[48] The ruins are attested by a Papal Bull of Anacletus II (1130–8). The text is published in Urlichs (1871), 147. On the later history of the idea of the Capitol see Saxl (1957), 200–14.

the relevant statue, thus warning the Romans to defend their imperial power.[49] The relentless efficiency of Roman rule over the vast expanse of the empire could in the twelfth century be explained only through magic. Yet such stories preserved the particular talismanic force the ancient Romans had attributed to the Capitol, through the cult of Jupiter Optimus Maximus, in assuring the empire's continuity.

Another twelfth-century text, the *Mirabilia urbis Romae* of Canon Benedict (which like that of Magister Gregorius, draws on some classical texts), described the Capitoline as *caput mundi*, where the consuls and senators had met to govern the world (3.7). More regular meeting places of the senate are overlooked, as the political and symbolic centres of Rome are conflated. In view of the symbolic significance of this hill, it is not surprising that when Romans of the twelfth century wanted to assert a civic power independent of the papacy, they chose for the site of their senate meetings not the curia down beside the ancient forum, but the Capitol (the forum was by this time completely desolate, while even the Capitol was on the very edge of the inhabited part of the city).[50] The popes, following Constantine's ecclesiastical foundations, had established themselves on the margins of the pagan city at the Lateran and Vatican.[51] Invoking an older tradition, those who sought to revive the Roman republic (though their political ambitions went no further than Rome itself) appropriated the ancient topographical symbol of the empire's power and permanence.

In the mid fourteenth century (at a time when the popes had abandoned Rome to the warring nobles, in favour of the security of French protection in Avignon), two rather different ceremonies, each claiming to revive ancient practices, suggest the continuing strength of the association between ancient Rome's potential for revival and this hill, the symbol of its eternity: the coronation of Petrarch as poet laureate in 1341 and Cola di Rienzo's assumption of the title of Tribunus Augustus and coronation in 1347. While the games of Domitian provided a precedent for the crowning of poets on the Capitoline, the tree used was probably oak rather than laurel; certainly Horace and Virgil were never

---

[49] Different versions of this story appear in a number of medieval sources. See Graf (1915), 148–61. Gibbon quotes this version in *Decline and Fall* Ch. 71.

[50] Gibbon's description of this new regime is quoted above. Cf. Krautheimer (1980) 197, 285–8.

[51] *Ibid.*, 3–31, 54–8.

(as Petrarch believed) crowned there – though each embraced the Capitol metaphorically, as we have seen. Yet Petrarch was convinced this was an ancient tradition, when, as he tells in his letters, the king of Naples invited him to receive a crown of laurel on the Capitol, in recognition of his unique contribution to Latin letters (*Fam.* 4.4).[52] On Easter day 1341, he was crowned in the Palazzo del Senatore on the Capitoline hill (where Cicero, he mistakenly thought, had once addressed Caesar) and was declared a citizen of Rome.[53] According to a contemporary description of the procession, he then recited a sonnet praising the Romans of antiquity, to which the assembly responded with shouts of: 'Long live the Capitol and the poet!'[54] Once again the flourishing of Latin poetry was intertwined with that of the Capitol.

This self-conscious revival of antiquity no doubt influenced Petrarch's contemporary, Cola di Rienzo, as scholars have often suggested.[55] The instigator of two short-lived uprisings (1347 and 1354) against the violent aristocratic domination of Rome, Cola was said to have been inspired to fight for more democratic government by the physical remains of Roman antiquity.[56] Assuming the title Tribune of Rome in 1347, he argued for a united Italy and the vindication of the ancient powers of the Roman people. It was on the Capitol that he published new laws for the good government of Rome (*Life* 1.6). He also appropriated the hill as seat of his regime (1.14). Later in the same year (15 August), he was crowned Tribunus Augustus on the Capitoline hill.[57] The Capitol stood for the legitimate power of the Roman people; through pseudo-antique ritual, Cola could be figured as part of the eternal political tradition of Rome. The steep staircase up the Capitoline to Santa Maria in Aracoeli, the only significant monument in the city known from the fourteenth century, was constructed in 1348 (a votive for delivery from the plague). As Krautheimer comments, the steps 'reflect the fantastic dream of Cola di Rienzo to establish a Roman

---

[52] Trapp suggests Petrarch himself probably solicited the invitation and discusses the sources, ancient and contemporary, on which Petrarch based his idea of coronation (1982), 93–130.

[53] The text of the oration written for the occasion is preserved (Latin in Petrarch (1874), 311–28; translation in Wilkins (1955), 300–13).

[54] For the description see Petrarch (1874), 20–1.

[55] See Saxl (1957), 202–3.

[56] *The Life of Cola di Rienzo* 1.1.

[57] Cf. Gregorovius (1898) XI, 283–7.

republic, superior to Emperor and Pope, with its seat on the Capitol from which the world was once ruled'.[58]

Though the papacy was firmly re-established in Rome by the start of the fifteenth century, the Capitol remained marginal and neglected for decades. We have seen something of the way Poggio used the ruins on the Capitol for a contemplation of fortune's vicissitudes, incidentally providing considerable detail on the extent of the remains. Flavio Biondo laments the sorry condition of the Capitol in *Roma instaurata* (1444–6): *pudet enim pigetque a Capitolio incipientem eius deformitatem referre*, 'Beginning my description from the Capitol, I am ashamed and sad to describe its ruined state.' He describes the splendours of the Capitol in antiquity (quoting Cicero, Virgil, Ammianus Marcellinus and Cassiodorus), then continues:

> nunc vero praeter latericiam domum a Bonifacio IX ruinis super-aedificatam qualem mediocris olim fastidisset Romanus cives usibus Senatoris et causidicorum deputatam, praeter Arae Coeli fratrum Beati Francisci ecclesiam in Feretrii Iovis templi fundamentis extructam, nihil habet is Capitolinus Tarpeiusve mons tantis olim aedificiis exornatus.

> Now, however, apart from the brick building constructed on ruins by Pope Boniface IX and (though such as once an ordinary Roman citizen would have despised) designated for the use of the Senator and advocates, and the church of the Ara Coeli of the friars of St Francis, built on the foundations of the temple of Jupiter Feretrius, that Capitoline or Tarpeian mount, once adorned with such great buildings, has nothing.   (73)

The Palazzo del Senatore remodelled under Pope Boniface (1389–1404) seems indeed to have been a utilitarian structure, fortified by towers and with little in the way of decoration.

A far more extensive material renewal of the Capitoline took place under Pope Nicholas V (1447–55), as part of an ambitious scheme of urban planning for the city of Rome. The Palazzo del Senatore was given a new façade and a new municipal palace was built, the Palazzo dei Conservatori. Here in 1474 Pope Sixtus IV (1471–84) established a collection of antiquities, including the bronze statues of the she-wolf and

---

[58] Krautheimer (1980), 228.

the Spinario, together with Samson's ball (an arm holding a globe thought to be part of a statue of Nero) and many other pieces which had previously been kept at the pope's Lateran palace.[59] The inscription read: SIXTUS IIII. PONT. MAX OB IMMENSAM BENIGNITATEM AENEAS INSIGNES STATUAS PRISCAE EXCELLENTIAE VIRTUTISQUE MONUMENTUM ROMANO POPULO UNDE EXORTAE FUERE RESTITUENDAS CONDONANDASQUE CENSUIT..., 'Sixtus IV, Pontifex Maximus, through his great goodness, has decided that the fine bronze statues – a reminder to the Roman people of ancient excellence and virtue – should be returned as a gift to the place whence they came.' As Stinger comments, these statues, in their position outside the Lateran, had symbolised the triumph of Christianity over pagan antiquity. Now, in a location seen as the centre and symbol of the pagan Roman empire, they were to function as inspiring reminders of the excellence and virtue of the ancient Romans. But, as the inscription emphasises, this was a role licensed by papal authority.[60]

Pope Paul III (1534–49) commissioned Michelangelo to redesign the Capitol, whose orientation towards the Campus Martius was now confirmed. In the centre of Michelangelo's square, on a base designed by the architect, was placed the equestrian statue of Marcus Aurelius also from the Lateran (for centuries thought to be a statue of Constantine and hence saved from destruction). On the base were inscribed the words: HANC PETUNT MIRACULA SEDEM, 'Wonders seek this home.'[61] The remains of antiquity are drawn back to the centre of the ancient city. Once again we see the vocabulary of the marvellous associated with the material manifestations of ancient Rome.[62] Yet, as Stinger observes: 'As these symbols of Roman triumph, power and majesty multiplied on the Capitoline, the Capitol's actual role in municipal government diminished.'[63] Papal authority over civic affairs became ever more assertive.

Papal generosity safely neutralised the Capitol's political charge for the next few centuries – though under French occupation the hill was

[59] Stinger (1985), 255–8.
[60] On the tensions between municipal Rome and the papacy, symbolised by the displacement of the municipal lion by the ancient Roman wolf, see Miglio (1982).
[61] Stinger (1985), 258.
[62] See Ch. 4, below.
[63] Stringer (1985), 256.

briefly adorned with a tree of liberty and in 1799 saw the performance of Voltaire's republican play *Le mort de César* (in which the bronze she-wolf was used as a prop).[64] The Capitol once again became a live political symbol in the late nineteenth century, with the unification of Italy. When Rome was finally wrested from the papacy to become the new capital in 1871, the city government proclaimed itself heir to Rome's ancient municipal traditions. The letters SPQR appeared on drain covers and Rome's mayors were listed in new Fasti. The ritual centres of the Christian city were de-emphasised. Instead, attention was focused on places associated with resistance to papal rule. Statues were erected to Giordano Bruno in the Campo de' Fiori and Cola di Rienzo on the Capitol, as well as to more recent heroes of the Risorgimento. Most strikingly, a vast monument to King Victor Emanuel II (begun in 1885 and completed in 1911) was constructed on the slope of the Capitoline facing north towards the Piazza del Popolo, the monument's vast size perhaps portending a renewal of Rome's imperial ambitions.[65]

The Capitoline hill, one of the symbols of Romanità most favoured by the Fascist regime, was among those parts of the city profoundly transformed under Mussolini. Urban planning projects of the regime were publicised along with other activities of the city government in a monthly journal entitled *Capitolium*, founded in 1925. When the bimillennium of Horace's birth was celebrated in 1935, as Saxl notes, stamps were issued showing the Capitol and the words *Stet Capitolium fulgens*, 'May the Capitol stand bright!' (Horace *Carm.* 3.3.42–3). When Mussolini himself spoke from the Capitol, hanging below him was a representation of the she-wolf with the same phrase from Horace (see Plate 4).[66] This hill with all its resonances could be seen as providing legitimacy for Mussolini's own imperial projects – a new Italian empire was declared in 1936.

A scheme to free the ancient Roman Capitol from the accretions of later ages was already envisaged in 1919 (before Mussolini came to power).[67] In 1925 Mussolini reasserted the importance of creating space around such ancient monuments as the Theatre of Marcellus, the Pantheon and the Capitol, as part of a project to make a new Rome equal

[64] Springer (1987), 34.
[65] Kostof (1973), 13, 20.
[66] Saxl (1957), 213 with Plates 142 b and c.
[67] Manacorda and Tamassia (1985), 57–8 and 171–4.

in size, order and power to that of the Augustan empire.[68] The memory of
intervening centuries, when Italy's military standing had not been so
high, was to be effaced. In work begun in 1926, virtually all buildings,
public and private, on the slopes of the Capitoline hill were destroyed,
under the direction of the indefatigable Antonio Muñoz (then Soprinten-
dente ai Monumenti di Lazio). An extensive justification for this policy,
written by G. B. Colonna, was published in *Capitolium* in 1940. He
argued for the need to liberate the Capitol and restore its ancient majesty
for the new imperial Rome. However, in addition to the 'groups of
horrible shacks which had been clambering up the rugged hill of the
Tarpeian rock like impertinent goats', as Colonna described them,
implicitly recalling the Monte Caprino of medieval times, it seems that
extensive remains of ancient Roman buildings were also destroyed.[69]
Muñoz insisted that they were modest structures without archaeological
significance.

Ambitious road-building plans (especially the clearing of Piazza
Venezia and the construction of Via del Mare) destroyed almost all the
buildings in the near vicinity of the hill. In 1939 the Via della Consolazione
and the Via del Foro Romano were begun, significantly enlarging an
existing road, thus covering over some of the most ancient parts of the
Roman forum and completing the isolation of the Capitol.[70] The
inauguration of these roads in 1942 might be seen as the culmination of
Rome's decapitation – a variation on the disembowellings (*sventramenti*)
deplored by critics of Mussolini's urban planning.[71] If Rome is the city of
empire, then imperial symbolism has been most intensely concentrated
on this hill. Even in the twentieth century, the ancient resonances of the
Capitol have played a significant part in determining the fortunes of this
particular area of the city of Rome.

[68] Translation in Scobie (1990), 9.
[69] 'Quel gregge di misere casupole aggrappate alla scabra roccia della Rupe Tarpea
come insolenti caprette', Colonna (1940), 521.
[70] Manacorda and Tamassia (1985), 171–4.
[71] See e.g. Cederna (1980).

4

The city of marvels

The most popular guide to the remains of ancient Rome in the middle ages (which appeared in a number of versions from the twelfth to the seventeenth centuries) was entitled the *Mirabilia urbis Romae – The Marvels of the City of Rome*. The Capitol in particular provoked the author to marvel. Perhaps recalling Virgil *Aeneid* 8.348, he writes: 'It was called the Golden Capitol because it surpassed all the realms of the world in wisdom and beauty' (3.7, Nichols tr.). Other writers, too, presented the city as a source of wonder. An English visitor to Rome in the twelfth century, Magister Gregorius, wrote a short account of what he had seen, which he termed a description *de mirabilibus urbis Romae que vel arte magica vel humano labore sunt condita*, 'of the marvels of the city of Rome which were created by magic or by human labour'. He begins his account by recommending to his readers the view of Rome from Monte Mario to the north. When he first saw it, he writes, his mind was struck by Lucan's description of Caesar's approach to Rome, after his years fighting in Gaul: *miratusque suae . . . moenia Romae*, 'he marvelled at the walls of his own Rome' (Lucan 3.90). The sense of wonder evoked by the city had a long history, as these twelfth-century authors were well aware; my principal concern in this chapter will be the sense of wonder the city evoked in ancient writers.

For them, as for Canon Benedict (the likely author of the *Mirabilia*) and Magister Gregorius, the amazement aroused by the city itself was intimately connected with awe at the power it had exercised over the rest of the world. Both the city in general and particular buildings within the city were perceived as manifestations of the unparalleled power of Rome and of Rome's rulers. Observers marvelled at the incredible size of

Rome's buildings, at the incomparable accumulation of precious materials from all over the world Rome ruled. But admiration was not the only response to the city's physical immensity. Rome's buildings could also seem monstrous – symbols of unparalleled luxury and exploitation. The latter part of this chapter will explore some of these darker reactions to the city.

Amazement

Ammianus Marcellinus, writing in the late fourth century, describes the visit to Rome of the emperor Constantius II, in 357 CE (16.10.13–17). For Constantius, emperor of the east, Rome was not a familiar city. Constantine had founded a new capital for the empire, Constantinople, in 324 (though even in the third century emperors had tended to keep their bases close to the frontiers, spending little time in Rome).[1] In Ammianus' narrative, Constantius is awestruck by the wonderful sights of the ancient capital city: the Forum Romanum, the Temple of Jupiter on the Capitol, the baths, the Colosseum, the Pantheon, the Temple of Rome, the Forum of Peace, the Theatre of Pompey and Trajan's Forum. Throughout his lengthy description Ammianus stresses the emperor's amazement at seeing Rome. Standing on the rostra he is stunned by the forum (obstipuit). 'On every side, wherever his eyes rested, he was overcome by the throng of marvels', miraculorum densitate praestrictus (16.10.13). The forum of Trajan makes the greatest impression upon the emperor, we are told – haerebat attonitus. Ammianus describes this as etiam numinum assessione mirabilem, 'a marvel even in the opinion of the gods' (16.10.15).[2]

Conveying the scale of Rome and its monuments poses a challenge for any writer. Ammianus compares the Pantheon to a city district in its scale: velut regionem. The baths, however, are built like whole provinces – lavacra in modum provinciarum exstructa. The Colosseum is so tall, human vision can scarcely make out the top. The Forum of Trajan, though, is felt to be beyond description or imitation – nec relatu effabiles, nec rursus mortalibus appetendos (16.10.15). The impossibility of describing Rome in general is summed up in the emperor's final complaint that

---

[1] According to Lactantius Mort. Pers. 27, the emperor Maximian never once visited Rome.
[2] On this passage and its context see Matthews (1986) and (1989), 231–5.

Fama is either incapable or malicious, for, though it always exaggerates everything else, it falls short in describing Rome (16.10.17).

Ammianus' description is interesting for what it leaves out as well as what it includes. A pagan, writing long after Constantine had begun the process of making the Roman empire Christian, Ammianus modelled his writing upon the work of Tacitus. Constantine had built vast Christian basilicas in Rome – rivalling in scale the basilicas of Trajan and other earlier emperors. Though far from the centre, these must surely have been visible to the visitor approaching the city, but Constantius' response to them is not thought worthy of mention by Ammianus.[3] In his text Rome maintains its pagan identity. Indeed, no building appears constructed later than the reign of Hadrian – some 200 years before Constantius' visit.

The most comprehensive descriptions of Rome and its fourteen regions to have survived date from the mid fourth century, a little before Ammianus was writing. The regionary catalogues, known as the *Notitia* and the *Curiosum*, furnish lists of the buildings and monuments of Rome.[4] The city contained, they claim, six obelisks, ten basilicas, eleven public baths, 22 equestrian statues, 80 golden statues, 36 triumphal arches, as well as 856 private baths, 254 bakeries and 46 brothels. Figures give an air of factual accuracy to the catalogues but, as Purcell comments: 'These texts are not valuable survivals of ancient bureaucracy; they are a stage in the development of the marvel literature of the city.'[5] It is perhaps legitimate to trace this preoccupation with number back at least to Augustan Rome, when some of the monuments set up in the city can be seen as making use of the 'rhetoric of number', in Purcell's phrase, to parade Rome's domination of the world: Agrippa's map in the Porticus Vipsania (which gave the dimensions of provinces conquered by Rome), the Golden Milestone in the Forum Romanum (which gave the distances from Rome to the principal cities of the empire),[6] not to mention Augustus' *Res gestae* (which lists the numbers of temples restored, colonies founded and wild beasts slaughtered for entertainment

---

[3] Though he does mention the basilica of Sicininus with reference to the events of 366 CE (27.3.13). On Ammianus' attitude to Christianity, see Matthews (1989), 445–51. On the well developed late antique tradition of pagan texts in praise of Rome, see Classen (1980).

[4] Texts to be found in Valentini and Zucchetti (1940), I 63–258.

[5] Purcell (1992), 425.

[6] Nicolet (1991), 103. Dio 54.8.4; Pliny *NH* 3.66.

under that emperor).[7] The dimensions of the empire were inscribed in the city of Rome.

The different strategies for describing the city deployed in fourth-century texts are also to be found in earlier descriptions of aspects of the city of Rome. Tacitus, of course, offers no description of the city comparable to that of Ammianus – Rome is assumed to be familiar to his urbane readers.[8] But other texts, such as the elder Pliny's *Naturalis historia*, seem readier to address a less sophisticated audience. Pliny's *Naturalis historia*, like the regionary catalogues, is often used by modern scholars as a mine of useful facts about the ancient city. What I want to emphasise here are the rhetorical strategies Pliny deploys in presenting a verbal picture of Rome. Among the most important passages in this context are *NH* 3.66–7 and 36.101–24.

One striking aspect of Pliny's descriptions of the city, in Book 3 in particular, is his emphasis on enumeration, an emphasis which foreshadows that of the fourth-century regionary catalogues.[9] The area surrounded by the walls in the 826th year of foundation of the city is 13 miles and 200 yards in circumference. It is divided into fourteen regions with 265 crossways with their guardian Lares. The more extensive description of Rome in Book 36 also includes many numbers: 250,000 can be seated in the Circus Maximus. Julius Caesar gave 1,000,000 sesterces merely for the ground on which his forum was to be built. Agrippa constructed 700 basins and 500 fountains as part of his refurbishment of the water supply system. The construction work for the most recent aqueduct, the Aqua Claudia, together with some associated projects, cost 350,000,000 sesterces.

This is one sense in which Rome outshines all rivals. Another strategy for conveying the city's unique status is to represent Rome as in itself equivalent to the entire world. As Pliny remarks: *universitate vero acervata et in quendam unum cumulum coiecta non alia magnitudo exurget quam si mundus alius quidam in uno loco narretur* – 'if all this were massed together and heaped up into one mound, its size would rise as great as if a whole other world were being described in one place'. The sum of Rome

---

[7] This development is extensively discussed by Nicolet (1991), 171–87.

[8] Cf. Rouveret (1991).

[9] Some of the numerical data in Pliny, according to Nicolet (1991), 101, are likely to have come from Agrippa's map and accompanying commentarii. Cf. Purcell (1992), esp. 423–6. On the rhetorical importance of number in Pliny's work, see also Conte (1994), 67–72.

is equivalent to another world, *mundus alius*. Earlier in the *Naturalis historia* (2.1), Pliny describes the world itself as *aeternum*, 'everlasting', and *immensum*, 'immeasurable', qualities he goes on to attribute to Rome. One could see the equivalence Pliny suggests between Rome and the world as another example of the play on the verbal resemblance between *urbs*, 'city' and *orbis*, 'world', which seems to appear first in Cicero and is repeatedly exploited in Augustan literature.[10] Ovid, for instance, with reference to the festival of the god Terminus, the divinity responsible for boundaries, comments: *Romanae spatium est urbis et orbis idem*, 'The world and the city of Rome occupy the same space' (*Fasti* 2.684).[11] Rome extends through the whole world and at the same time all the world is concentrated in Rome.[12]

In some senses, all the world *was* represented physically in Rome. Pliny earlier describes the aim of Agrippa's map 'to show the entire world to the *urbs*'.[13] The world was on display in the city in other ways, too. At *NH* 3.54, Pliny observes that anything that is produced on earth can be bought in Rome.[14] And fragments of Rome's empire were everywhere visible: obelisks from Egypt (mostly brought back after Augustus' conquest of the province),[15] architectural decorations taken from eastern temples, not to mention the miscellaneous population of the city – Rome's greatest marvel, according to Ludwig Freidländer. This absorption of the world came about through conquest, and Pliny keeps constantly before his reader's mind the status of Rome as world-conqueror. The buildings of the city are another arena in which Rome outdoes all other nations: *sic quoque terrarum orbem victum ostendere*, 'thus also is the rest of the world shown to be defeated' (36.101). The miraculous constructions of the Romans are themselves described as *invicta*, 'unconquered' (36.121 on aqueducts).

[10] Cf. Nicolet (1991), 114.
[11] Cf. Ovid's description of Rome celebrating Germanicus' triumph: *quaeque capit vastis inmensum moenibus orbem, | hospitiis Romam vix habuisse locum*, 'Rome, embracing the measureless world within her great walls, hardly had space for all her guests' (*Ex Ponto* 2.1.23–4).
[12] This idea recurs in many later references to the city. Cf. e.g. Rutilius Namatianus *De reditu* 1.65–6.
[13] The linguistic parallel between Pliny and Ovid is noted by Nicolet (1991), 110–11, who wonders if a similar word play might not have been found in Agrippa's commentarii.
[14] Cf. *NH* 11.240. For an examination of this idea see Gowers (1993), esp.18–19.
[15] These are listed by Pliny, *NH* 36.70–4.

The lengthy passage describing the city in *NH* 36 begins with an attempt to convey the sense of amazement which Rome evokes.[16] It is now the moment, writes Pliny, to turn to *urbis nostrae miracula* (36.101). This sense of wonderment pervades his description of the city – *miracula* and cognate words are used repeatedly.[17] Foremost among these marvels, he lists the Basilica of Paullus[18] – *columnis e Phrygibus ... mirabilem*, 'remarkable for its Phrygian columns' – the forum of divine Augustus and the Emperor Vespasian's Temple of Peace. These buildings are *pulcherrima operum quae umquam vidit orbis*, 'the most beautiful buildings the world has ever seen' (36.102).

This celebratory description might seem a response to warm the hearts of emperors who paraded their concern to endow the Roman people with appropriate public monuments.[19] The physical appearance of republican Rome had been seen as unworthy of its status as capital of a world empire – or so Livy suggests, writing under Augustus, the most renowned beautifier of the city. A critical assessment of Rome's physical appearance, for instance, is put in the mouths of some Macedonian Greeks visiting in the early second century BCE: 'Some made fun of the Romans' traditions and customs, others of their accomplishments, others of individual members of the aristocracy, others of the appearance of the city itself, not yet beautiful in either public or private domains' (40.5.7). Augustus' enhancement of the city is praised for its appropriateness by Vitruvius, who compliments the emperor for his concern with the provision of suitable public buildings (*opportunitate publicorum aedificiorum*) with the effect that: 'the state was not only made greater through you by its new provinces but the majesty of the empire also was expressed through the eminent dignity of its public buildings' (1. pr.2).[20]

But Pliny has little to say about suitability of imperial constructions

---

[16] Though it is notable that Pliny is preoccupied with the marvellous throughout the *NH*, as Conte notes (1994), 86.

[17] *basilicam ... mirabilem* (102), *senes ... mirabantur* (104), *uni comparanda miraculo* (109), *quid enim miretur ... ?* (118), *invicta miracula* (121), *nil magis mirandum* (123). Cf. 3.67 – *aggere Tarquini Superbi inter prima opere mirabili*. Conte (1994), 79–87 discusses the importance of the marvellous as a category in *NH*.

[18] The identification of this building has recently been the subject of debate. See Patterson (1992), 193.

[19] Cf. e.g. *Res gestae* 19–21; Suet. *Aug.* 28. On imperial self-presentation through the medium of building see Zanker (1988), Edwards (1993), 163–72 and Elsner (1994).

[20] *Ut civitas per te non solum provinciis esset aucta, verum etiam ut maiestas imperii publicorum aedificiorum egregias haberet auctoritates.*

and, on closer inspection, the emphases of his account may strike us as rather curious. He tells us almost nothing about the three buildings which he terms the most beautiful in the world. The Basilica Paulli has some wonderful Phrygian columns (he does not say how many); the Forum of Augustus and the Temple of Peace appear to have no distinguishing features whatsoever.[21] Is it just that these buildings are ineffably beautiful? Or are they perhaps too familiar to need any description? I shall return below to this strange silence.

Luxury

Pliny then goes on to tell his readers about a number of other amazing constructions, which he describes in rather more detail: Agrippa's *diribitorium* (whose roof is a great feat of engineering), Julius Caesar's Forum (for which the land alone cost 1,000,000 sesterces). But at this point there is a disconcerting swerve in Pliny's account. The next building listed is the private house of Clodius (the tribune of the plebs made notorious by his enemy Cicero) which Pliny alleges cost 14,800,000 sesterces – a piece of expenditure which he compares with 'the mad schemes of kings' – *non secus ac insaniam regum miror* (103). This too is one of the marvels of Rome – but one whose moral connotations are decidedly shady.

Thereafter all the buildings Pliny mentions in any detail are ones he disapproves of. While one sentence was enough to tell of the most beautiful buildings of the city, whole paragraphs are required to describe structures which are manifestations of perverse morals. He tells of increasingly luxurious houses, equipped with vast quantities of marble and innumerable paintings, and concludes: 'We may be sure that fires punish our luxury' (110). The vast palaces of the emperors Gaius and Nero come in for extensive criticism, though little is said about these structures beyond the fact that their scale outdoes that of all other luxurious houses put together – again the language of conquest is used, *vicerunt*. This time, however, it is Romans who are the vanquished as well as the victors.

The buildings described in greatest detail are two structures long

---

[21] Elsewhere Pliny does describe some of the works of art on view in the latter buildings: Forum Augustum: *NH* 7.183; 16.191; 34.48; 35.27, 93–4; Temple of Peace: *NH* 34.84; 35.74, 102, 109; 36.27, 58.

vanished in Pliny's time: the temporary theatre built by Marcus Aemilius
Scaurus and the revolving theatres (which converted into an amphitheatre)
built by Gaius Scribonius Curio, both put up in the late republic.[22] Only
now are we given a building's full particulars: the theatre of Scaurus had
a stage arranged in three storeys with 360 columns, the lowest of marble,
the middle one of glass, the top storey of gilded planks. The columns of
the lowest storey were 38 feet high. There were 3,000 bronze statues. In
the case of Curio's revolving theatres, we are told all about the system of
pivots – a device of extraordinary ingenuity.

More space, however, is devoted to invective against the immorality of
these buildings. Scaurus' theatre is alleged to have caused more harm
than the proscriptions of his stepfather Sulla (money from the proscriptions,
Pliny claims, paid for all this finery). Here again we find the motif of all
the world gathered in Rome – 'things gathered from all the world',
convectis ex orbe terrarum rebus (116) – to decorate Scaurus' theatre. But,
although this accumulation is another indication of Rome's power, Pliny
is relieved at its destruction by fire. Curio's device Pliny attacks for the
danger in which it placed the spectators. 'Here we have the nation that
has conquered the earth, that has subdued the whole world, that
distributes tribes and kingdoms, that despatches its dictates to foreign
kingdoms, that is heaven's representative among mankind, so to speak,
swaying on a contraption and applauding its own danger' (118). The
Roman people were more at risk, he claims, than the gladiators they were
watching. Indeed, it was the audience which became the real spectacle
(119). The disastrous collapse of a building set up for public entertainment
was not unknown in the early principate. Tacitus tells of a catastrophe of
this kind at Fidenae, not far from Rome (*Ann.* 4.62–3). Curio's
theatres-cum-amphitheatre, however, seem to have functioned perfectly
well. Pliny must be satisfied with imagining what *might* have happened.

Pliny's account of the city of Rome, then, is full of moralising
judgements which are inseparable from his comments on the aesthetic
value of buildings. What is it that makes him approve of some buildings
and disapprove of others? First, it seems clear that he disapproves of
lavish buildings put up for private enjoyment. At 36.103, for instance, we
move from praise of Caesar's generosity in building a forum to criticism
of Clodius' extravagance in spending on a private house. Similarly, Pliny

---

[22] Scaurus' theatre is a favourite topic in Pliny *NH*. Cf. 36.5, 50, 189.

criticises the palaces of Gaius and Nero – structures devoted to private pleasure (111–12). Earlier in Book 36 (48–9), he comments disapprovingly on the use of luxurious materials in private houses under the republic.

This would seem to correspond to the distinction famously adduced by Cicero: *odit populus Romanus privatam luxuriam, publicam magnificentiam diligit*, 'The Roman people hate private luxury but love public magnificence' (*Mur.* 76). However, from his attack on the buildings erected by Scaurus and Curio, Pliny also seems to disapprove of some buildings put up for the pleasure of the Roman people, particularly when the personal advancement of the provider is also an objective (36.120). Earlier in Book 36, he comments that public routes are often the commonest ones by which vices creep in – *aut qua magis via inrepunt vitia quam publica?* (*NH* 36.5). In part Pliny's disapproval may relate to the status of the particular builders; at several points in his account we are reminded that vast building projects are normally associated with kings (referring to Clodius' luxurious house and Curio's twin theatres 36.104, 120). Lavish public building is an index of excessive political ambition. But it is not at all clear that such buildings if constructed by legitimate rulers would be morally satisfactory.

At this point, we return to those buildings Pliny described as *pulcherrima* – the Basilica Paulli, the Forum of Augustus and Vespasian's Temple of Peace. These would seem to fall into the category of buildings for public use erected by good rulers (the version of the Basilica Paulli visible in Pliny's Rome was financed by Augustus, in association with friends of Paullus, after a fire in 14 BCE).[23] Yet Pliny's reticence on the details of, for instance, the Forum of Augustus may be an indication that he is not altogether at ease with expenditure on public building even by emperors.[24] Why should he hesitate to describe the most beautiful buildings in Rome? The materials of which they were made are relevant here. The use of marble for any purpose is morally problematic within the overall scheme of the *Naturalis historia*. Pliny repeatedly castigates the quarrying of marble and its transport overseas as horribly unnatural activities: 'We remove barriers created to serve as the boundaries between nations, and ships are built especially for marble. And so over the waves of the sea, Nature's wildest element, mountain ranges are transported to and fro . . . When we hear of the prices paid for these

---

[23] See Dio 54.24.3 and the discussion in Steinby (1993–), *s.v.*
[24] Cf. Edwards (1993), 157.

vessels, when we see the masses of marble that are being conveyed or hauled, we should each of us reflect and at the same time think how much more happily people live without them' (*NH* 36.2–3).[25] To describe the Forum of Augustus or the Temple of Peace in any detail, to list the varieties of marble used, the number of columns and statues, would inevitably reveal their similarity to the reviled buildings of Scaurus and Curio. To describe their beauty would be to compromise it.

This reticence is one of the strategies Pliny adopts in his struggle to rescue his contemporaries from the inexorable logic of the myth of Roman decline, according to which earlier Romans are always more virtuous than later ones. Pliny's difficulty is at its most obvious in the conclusion to his discussion of the buildings of Scaurus and Curio. Here Pliny claims, in an inversion of the more usual Roman moral nostalgia, that in comparison with these men of the late republic, it is those of his own day who should be seen as *maiores* (117), since, though born in a later age, they excel their predecessors in morals – *moribus*. Thus by becoming the metaphorical *maiores* of Scaurus and Curio, Augustus and Vespasian can be presented as innocent of any charge of building to corrupt.

But Pliny's extensive criticism of luxurious builders – Gaius and Nero, as well as Scaurus and Curio – is more than just an indictment of the lowest ebb of Roman morals. This kind of criticism of Roman luxury can be seen as fulfilling a number of functions. The critic displays his own moral superiority. But at the same time the wealth and power of Rome receive further advertisement.[26]

Sewers, aqueducts, tyrants

Finally let us look at two categories of structure which do seem to be fully approved by Pliny *and* are described in considerable detail: sewers and aqueducts. To express proper admiration for the sewers is itself a sign of superior morals – only in the idealised past were they fully admired (104), alleges Pliny. He praises their immense strength and durability: they are 700 years old and have withstood earthquakes.[27] The aqueducts are even

---

[25] Cf. *NH* 12.1–2. These passages are discussed by Wallace-Hadrill (1990).
[26] Cf. Gowers (1993), 21.
[27] The original purpose of Rome's sewer system was probably to drain low-lying areas of the city, rather than to dispose of waste. The Cloaca Maxima was not enclosed until the late republic.

more impressive (121–4). We are given as many details of Agrippa's work on the water supply as we are even of Scaurus' theatre. The most recent among the aqueducts, completed by the emperor Claudius, are described as more admirable than anything in the world (123).

There are several reasons why sewers and aqueducts might be felt worthy of unqualified approval. For one thing, unlike so many features of Rome which could be seen as derived from the Greek east, these kinds of public structures were felt to be distinctively Roman. Frontinus, the official responsible for aqueducts under Nerva, commented in his treatise on the subject: *tot aquarum tam multis necessariis molibus pyramidas videlicet otiosas compares aut cetera inertia sed fama celebrata opera Graecorum*, 'With such an array of indispensable structures carrying so many waters, compare, if you will, the idle pyramids or the useless, though famous, works of the Greeks!' (*Aq.* 1.16).[28] Writing in the time of Augustus, the Greek Dionysius of Halicarnassus selected sewers, aqueducts and roads as the most magnificent of Rome's works, 'where the greatness of the empire is best seen' (3.67.5).

Sewers and aqueducts could also be distinguished from other public works on the grounds of their immense utility. We might compare Cicero's comment that utilitarian public buildings, such as walls and aqueducts, are more to be praised than temples and theatres:

> atque etiam illae impensae meliores, muri, navalia, portus, aquarum ductus omniaque, quae ad usum rei publicae pertinent. quamquam quod praesens tamquam in manum datur, iucundius est; tamen haec in posterum gratiora. theatra, porticus, nova templa, verecundius reprehendo propter Pompeium, sed doctissimi non probant.

> Again the expenditure of money is better justified when it is made for walls, docks, harbours, aqueducts and all those works which are of service to the community. There is, to be sure, more of present satisfaction in what is handed out, like cash down; nevertheless public improvements win us greater gratitude with posterity. Out of respect for Pompey, I am rather diffident about expressing any criticism of theatres, colonnades and new temples; and yet the greatest philosophers do not approve of them.   (*Off.* 2.60)

[28] Pliny also feels the need to denigrate the pyramids, in comparison with Roman public buildings (*NH* 36.103). Earlier, at 36.75, he terms them *pecuniae otiosa ac stulta ostentatio*.

Pliny too stresses utility in his praise of Roman water technology.

Pliny's anxieties about buildings, as we have seen, also relate to materials. Aqueducts and, especially, sewers are relatively free of columns, statues and marble decoration in general. What is astonishing about them is rather the immense amount of human labour needed to create them. Pliny writes of Claudius' attempt to drain the Fucine Lake, that it involved indescribable expenditure and labour. Solid rock had to be cut away and work on tunnels was carried out in darkness – *quae neque concipi animo nisi ab iis qui videre neque enarrari humano sermone possunt,* 'which cannot be imagined or described in human speech except by those who actually saw it' (124). Once again we should notice that the immensity of Roman public works eludes description.

The vast amount of labour needed for the construction of the sewers under King Tarquin in the sixth century BCE is also emphasised. In those early days available slave-labour was not sufficient to sustain great public works. Instead, citizens were obliged to do the work, which was so onerous, Pliny alleges, that many committed suicide to escape it. Tarquin devised a remedy for this – *novum, inexcogitatum antea posteaque,* 'new and untried previously or thereafter'. He had the bodies of those who had killed themselves crucified so that the others, horrified by the shame attached to this penalty, would not follow their example (36.107–8). Roman citizens are first exploited then crucified (a punishment normally associated with slaves). This is, of course, the act of a tyrant. Pliny is not the only writer to perceive a connection between vast public works projects and tyranny. Livy, too, in his history of early Rome relates that *plebs gravabatur,* 'the common people were oppressed' by the building of the sewers (1.56) – though there is no mention of the crucifixion story. In rousing the Roman people against the Tarquins, Livy's Brutus is made to remind them among other things of the pride of the king and the wretched state of the plebs: *in fossas cloacasque exhauriendas demersae; Romanos homines, victores omnium circa populorum, opifices et lapicidas pro bellatoribus factos,* 'who were plunged into ditches and sewers and made to clear them out. The men of Rome, he said, the conquerors of all the nations round about had been transformed from warriors into artisans and stone-cutters' (1.59.9). The genesis of Rome's sewers is decidedly sinister. And we may wonder whether the marvels of Rome's sewer-system would have been possible without such exploitation. The sewers, then, can perhaps be seen as a residue of tyranny, repressed in Rome's subconscious.[29]

But at least aqueducts, built under the republic and the principate, can be praised without reservation, we might imagine. Both Pliny and Livy point to the use of citizen labour in the construction of the sewers – implicitly there is a contrast with the aqueducts. But does the substitution of slave labour for citizen labour really make the public works of emperors unproblematic? How far might reflections on Rome's sewers affect our view of the aqueducts too, that other system of public works so often coupled with them and, in a sense, their mirror image? There is something awesome about the power required to build on this scale.

At the beginning of Book 36, Pliny comments, 'All that we have considered in previous volumes can be thought of as created for the benefit of human kind. Mountains, however, were made by Nature for itself to serve as a kind of structure for holding together the inner parts of the earth and at the same time to enable the control of violent rivers, the calming of great waves on the sea and thus to curb the most unquiet of elements with the hardest part of nature's substance.' He goes on to castigate the disruption to these great bulwarks of nature caused by marble-quarrying. Pliny describes the quest for marble as *deliciarum causa*, 'for pleasure'; the provision of water supplies he treats as motivated by much higher aims. Yet the effect on the mountains is the same, and the language used to describe the great feats of engineering involved in building the aqueducts is curiously similar to the language Pliny uses to describe the disruptions to nature caused by marble quarrying.[30] Once again Pliny's avowed purpose seems to be undermined by his language.

Roman writers used a variety of strategies to convey the marvellous immensity of the city of Rome. We have seen how both Ammianus in the fourth century and Pliny in the first stress scale, number, and the senses in which Rome can be seen as incorporating the world. But there are some important differences between their approaches to the city. The Greek-born Ammianus, though he presents himself as writing in the classical Roman tradition, expresses, through the figure of the emperor Constantius, detailed and unqualified admiration for Rome's physical fabric. The

---

[29] The sewers have also been seen as the bowels of the city. For an exploration of this bodily metaphor, see Gowers (1993),14–15 and (1995).

[30] Compare 36.1–2 (on marble) with 121 and 124 (on aqueducts).

buildings of the early principate – and, as I mentioned earlier, he refers to none later than the emperor Hadrian – were a focus for Ammianus' nostalgia for pagan Rome and for Rome as the centre of power. The responses of Pliny and other educated Romans who lived under the early principate were more complex. The buildings of Rome, for them as for Ammianus, were a reminder of the power of Rome and Rome's emperors. But, as inhabitants of a post-republican moral discourse, they could not feel at ease with these buildings. Even sewers and aqueducts – those most wholesome products of Roman engineering – could take on a sinister aspect – while the most beautiful buildings of Rome had the effect of leaving Pliny conveniently speechless.

5

The city of exiles

One of Rome's greatest marvels, as we have seen, was its enormous and multifarious population. How many Romans were born in Rome? Seneca, in the *Ad Helviam* (written to console his mother when he himself was exiled), observes that Rome is a city full of exiles:

> 'carere patria intolerabile est.' aspice agedum hanc frequentiam, cui vix urbis immensae tecta sufficiunt; maxima pars istius turbae patria caret. ex municipiis et coloniis suis, ex toto denique orbe terrarum confluxerunt ... iube istos omnes ad nomen citari et 'unde domo' quisque sit quaere. videbis maiorem partem esse, quae relictis sedibus suis venerit in maximam quidem ac pulcherrimam urbem, non tamen suam.

> 'To be absent from one's native land is unbearable', you say. Come now, observe this mass of people for whom the buildings of this great city scarcely afford sufficient space. A great part of this crowd are absent from their native lands. They flock from towns and colonies, from every part of the world indeed ... Give orders that each be called by name and asked 'Where do you come from?' You shall see that the greater part have left behind the place where they were born and come to this city, the greatest, the most beautiful city perhaps, but not their own. (*Helv.* 6.2–3)

For the Stoic, of course, even exile is not an impediment to living the good life; the *Ad Helviam* strives to make little of the author's isolation on Corsica.[1] Yet Seneca, in this same passage, betrays some sympathy for

---

[1] On Seneca's exile, see Griffin (1976), 59–63.

those who, in coming to Rome, have taken on voluntary exile from their native lands (the fate of his own family, indeed, drawn to Rome from Spain); while some seek a rich field for vice, others are attracted by the prospect of a wider scope for their virtues. This treatise then perhaps hints at the alienation experienced by the exile, the stranger seeking a new identity in that greatest and most beautiful city, Rome.[2]

The perspective of those new to the empire's capital is, however, rarely represented in Latin literature – though Ovid's book, anthropomorphised in *Tristia* 3.1, mimics the astonishment of the provincial tourist on a first visit to the capital. Seneca writes of those who abandon their own *patria* to come to Rome; he himself was born in the Spanish city of Corduba but, in the logic of his treatise, Rome is the *patria* he has lost through exile. Those other eloquent Romans whose laments for their lost city will be examined below, Cicero and Ovid, were born not in Rome but in Arpinum and Sulmo, respectively. Both write fondly of their native towns but it is Rome the *maxima ... ac pulcherrima urbs* which has the stronger claim.[3] Perhaps for these Romans especially exile from Rome raised questions about what it was to be Roman.

Many prominent Romans spent periods in exile.[4] Many more must have feared such a fate. Exile itself brought disgrace, often poverty and always uncertainty as to when or indeed whether the exile would ever see Rome again. This last question was an issue for others besides exiles; elite Romans frequently spent long periods away for education in Greece and Asia Minor but also to serve in the army or imperial administration. The present discussion will not be confined to writing about exile but will also consider writing associated with other forms of prolonged absence from the city.

There was in Rome a literary tradition of responses to exile. Cicero, in the *Tusculans*, draws on examples from literary works and the lives of philosophers for arguments to console the exile (5.106–9). Livy puts into the mouth of Camillus, who had been driven out of Rome, phrases

---

[2] On attitudes to exile in antiquity, see André and Baslez (1993), 527–37; Balsdon (1979), 102–15.
[3] Cicero on dual allegiance: *Leg.* 2.5. Ovid on Sulmo: *Pont.* 1.8.41–2.
[4] Periods of exile were regularly imposed on elite Romans as punishment for certain criminal offences. The mildest form this might take was exclusion from the city of Rome. In its most severe form, *deportatio*, the exile was confined to a specified place and suffered loss of property and citizenship.

reminiscent of Cicero.[5] Ovid, himself in exile on the bleak shore of the
Black Sea, echoes Cicero's writings from exile.[6] Seneca in Corsica seems
to have consoled himself by reading Ovid.[7] The act of leaving Rome (and
also of returning to Rome after a prolonged absence) is repeatedly
constructed by Roman authors as a moment of intense emotional
response to the city itself. In contrast to Cicero and Ovid, who present
themselves as deeply attached to Rome, the response to the city from the
figure of Umbricius, poised to leave Rome for good of his own accord in
Juvenal's third Satire, seems one of almost unmitigated hostility.
Nevertheless, Juvenal's satire needs to be looked at in the tradition of
exile literature, for it is, I shall suggest, a mirror-image of Ovid's lament
for Rome. Like Ovid, Juvenal may be seen as evoking the Virgilian
account of Aeneas' departure from Troy – a crucial moment in the
teleological narrative of the *Aeneid* which culminates in the foundation of
Rome itself. Rome was founded by exiles, as Seneca goes on to comment
in the *Ad Helviam* (7.7); exile, alienation, displacement were associated
with Rome from before the beginning of the city's history.[8]

This chapter will end by exploring parallels between the longing for
Rome on the part of exiled Romans and on the part of visitors and
would-be visitors in later centuries. With the establishment of Christianity,
the Latin term *peregrini*, 'foreigners', came to mean specifically pilgrims,
those who travelled to Rome for religious purposes. Here too Rome
functioned as a second but more powerful *patria*, this time to Christendom
rather than to the inhabitants of the Roman empire. But the new Rome
did not entirely displace the old; Catholic Rome and the Rome of pagan
antiquity, their material aspects inextricably intertwined, coexisted uneasily.

Petrarch, rare among his contemporaries, interested himself specifically
in the pagan resonances of the city. Visiting Rome in 1337, he was, he
writes, astounded by the Romans' ignorance about their own city: 'Who
are more ignorant about Roman affairs than the Roman citizens? Sadly

---

[5] Cf. Ogilvie (1970) *ad* Livy 5.54.
[6] Cf. Nagle (1980), 35.
[7] Griffin (1976), 62.
[8] One might compare here Livy's repeated insistence on the heterogeneity of Rome's
population in the earliest books of his history (cf. e.g. 1.8.5–6 on Romulus' asylum
which attracts a miscellaneous rabble from the surrounding territories). In the
Aeneid too, Rome is settled successively by exiles: Saturn, Evander, Aeneas and
Romulus (8.320).

do I say that nowhere is Rome less known than in Rome.'[9] We may perhaps detect here an echo of Cicero (an author much admired by Petrarch), who, in the *Academica*, praised the learned Varro for rescuing the Romans from their profound ignorance of their own city.[10] Rome was always a place where the outsider might become more Roman than the Romans. Through his reading and his writing, Petrarch had first come to know the city. Born in Florence, he was later to be given, in the ceremony on the Capitol discussed in Chapter 3 above, honorary citizenship of Rome.

'O Rome! my country! city of the soul!' apostrophises Lord Byron in *Childe Harold's Pilgrimage* (IV 78). The romantic desire to savour the unbridgeable gulf between the present and the past found Rome and its ruins especially congenial. Rome suggested tantalisingly a sense of belonging that could never be fully realised. The American Nathaniel Hawthorne, in his novel *The Marble Faun* (1860), develops the idea of Rome as home. On leaving Rome, he writes, we find 'our heart strings have mysteriously attached themselves to the Eternal City and are drawing us thitherward again, as if it were more familiar, more intimately our home, than even the spot where we were born' (II 373). Significantly this sense of attachment is at its most intense once the visitor has left. While in the city, Hawthorne's protagonists seem more ambivalent in their responses.

Protestant visitors particularly would in their writings detail at length the curious customs of the modern Romans, their excessive passions, their superstitious religion and, in general, the strange experiences attendant on travel in a foreign land.[11] Yet while such visitors might despise the modern Romans, many still identified with the Romans of antiquity, known to them from earliest youth through decades of reading. Eustace, in his often reprinted *Classical Tour through Italy* of 1812, observes, 'one might almost say of every school boy not insensible to the sweets of his first studies, that he becomes in feelings and sentiment, perhaps even in language, a Roman'.[12] For many others besides Byron,

---

[9] Petrarch (1975) 6.2, p. 293.
[10] *Acad.* 1.9, quoted above p. 16. For Petrarch's knowledge of *Acad.*, see *Fam.* 24.4, addressed to Cicero.
[11] Cf. Pemble (1987), 173, 211–27; Varriano (1991), 8; Boyle (1991), 482; McGowan (1994), 246–7.
[12] Eustace (1821), I 57. Eustace himself was Roman Catholic but the majority of those for whom he wrote will have been Protestant.

Rome was a second *patria*, though one which was never fully attainable. The concerns of these later texts can, I hope, be made to highlight the preoccupation of Roman writers with what it means to be a Roman and what it means to be a stranger, an alien, whether in exile or in Rome itself.

Desiring Rome

Earlier chapters have considered some of the ways in which Cicero deploys references to Rome and its buildings in his speeches and philosophical texts. Cicero's correspondence documents various periods spent far away from Rome: as an exile in 58 BCE (following his role in the suppression of the Catilinarian conspiracy of 63), as governor of Cilicia in 51–50 BCE and travelling in Greece 49–48. Cicero's letters from exile are among his least forthcoming; excluded from Roman political life, the identity of the once voluble Cicero is somehow compromised. His letters are largely composed of complaints relating to the ill-treatment he had received from colleagues and the absence of friends and family, while the letters he has received are, he writes, blotted with his own tears (*Fam.* 9.1).[13]

Cicero's eloquence is, however, restored with his return to Rome. A letter to Atticus (73.5) describes his return from exile, while the same scene is presented more colourfully in the speech against Piso:

> unus ille dies mihi quidem immortalitatis instar fuit, quo in patriam redii, cum senatum egressum vidi populumque universum, cum mihi ipsa Roma prope convolsa sedibus suis ad complectendum conservatorem suum progredi visa est; quae me ita accepit, ut non modo omnium generum, aetatum, ordinum omnes viri ac mulieres omnis fortunae ac loci, sed etiam moenia ipsa viderentur et tecta urbis ac templa laetari.

> The actual day, when I returned to my homeland, was for me like an apotheosis. I saw the senate come out and the whole people. Indeed it seemed to me that Rome herself, risen up from her foundations, had come out to embrace her protector. Such was her welcome that I felt not only all manners, ages and ranks of men and women of every walk

---

[13] *Fam.* 6–10 (Shackleton Bailey numbering); *Att.* 46–73.

of life were rejoicing but even the walls themselves and the houses and
temples of the city.   (*In Pisonem* 52)

Cicero returns in triumph, vindicated by popular approval – the moment
is portrayed with hyperbolic imagery calculated to maximise the
discomfiture of Piso and others who had collaborated in Cicero's exile.
Cicero claimed to have rescued not only the citizens of Rome from the
rapacious followers of Catiline, but also the fabric of the city from their
plans for arson. Rome personified rises up to embrace her defender.

This is the first extant of many extended personifications of Rome
(though Cicero's fourth Catilinarian had also suggested a figure of Rome
supplicating the senate for protection, *Cat.* 4.18). The city, as we shall see,
was to take on a range of feminine forms in Latin literature. Lucan
presents Rome as accosting Caesar as he approaches the Rubicon
(1.185–92).[14] The figure of Rome in his poem recalls the mother of
Coriolanus whom Livy presents as coming out to dissuade her son from
attacking the city (2.40). Livy's version of the story elides Rome and
mother, as Veturia is made to say to her son: *potuisti populari hanc terram
quae te genuit atque aluit?* 'Did you feel able to devastate this land which
bore and raised you?'[15] The most extended personifications of Rome,
however, date from the fourth and fifth centuries. Claudian's Rome
beseeches help from Stilicho and Honorius.[16] Here Rome is explicitly
referred to as *parens* (*Cons. Hon.* VI 362). However, as we shall see below,
Rome in female form need not always be figured as mother.

Cicero's letters during his period as governor of Cilicia, a remote and
rugged province, are more explicitly charged than his letters from exile
with feeling for Rome itself. In a letter to Caelius of April 50 BCE, he
writes: *mirum me desiderium tenet urbis, incredibile meorum atque in
primis tui,* 'I am possessed by an overwhelming longing for the city and an
incredible longing for my friends, you above all' (*Fam.* 90.1), words
which are virtually echoed – Cicero is again possessed by a *mirum
desiderium* for the city and for his friends – in 93.3, also to Caelius. In a

---

[14] On this passage see Feeney (1991), 292–4.
[15] For an illuminating discussion of this see Bonjour (1975b), who emphasises the
parallels between Livy's Coriolanus and the historical figures of Marius and Caesar.
Livy also makes Camillus speak of Rome as *mater* (5.54.2).
[16] Cf. Cameron (1970), ch.12. On personifications of Rome in general, see Mellor
(1981), 1004–10, 1024. An antique statue of Roma is visible directly beneath
Mussolini in Plate 4.

later letter, he advises Caelius: *urbem, urbem, mi Rufe, cole et in ista luce vive. omnis peregrinatio . . . obscura et sordida est iis, quorum industria Romae potest illustris esse*, 'The city, the city, my Rufus, is what you must cultivate. In the city's brilliance you must live. All time abroad brings only wretched obscurity for those whose achievements can shine in Rome' (95.1). These passages were appropriated centuries later by foreigners, seeking to express their own feelings for Rome. Chateaubriand contrasts the physical appearance of the Campagna unfavourably with that of the area around Naples. Yet it is Rome which moves him more: 'One becomes marvellously attached to that famous territory: two thousand years ago Cicero believed himself exiled beneath the skies of Asia and wrote to his friends: *Urbem, mi Rufe, cole et in ista luce vive*. The attraction of fair Ausonia is still the same.'[17]

For Cicero *peregrinatio* may turn the traveller into a *peregrinus* in his own country (thus perhaps may Cicero's writings from exile have a particular appeal for the non-Roman). Cicero goes on to demand the latest news from Caelius so that on his return he will not be a stranger in Rome: *ne plane hospes veniam* (95.1). Cicero's fear of being a stranger, an outsider (perhaps the more understandable in one whose enemies mocked him for coming from Arpinum rather than Rome) foreshadows a passage (written some five years later) in the *Academica*, discussed above; the great scholar Varro is congratulated for offering, through his books, the means to give Romans true knowledge of Rome and thus no longer to wander like strangers in their own city. Even in his private correspondence, being Roman for Cicero is, if somewhat ironically, a matter of knowledge.

Wherever I roam . . .

Ovid's *Tristia* and *Ex Ponto*, written in exile in Tomis on the Black Sea, echo Cicero's writings from exile, for they too are stained with tears.[18] Ovid had been banished from Rome by Augustus in 8 BCE because of what he terms *carmen et error*, 'a poem and an indiscretion' (*Tristia* 2.207).[19] He spent the rest of his life in exile in Tomis. Many of the poems

---

[17] Letter to M. de Fontanes, January 1804.
[18] Cf. Nagle (1980), 33–5. E.g. *Tristia* 3.1.15. Hinds (1985), 14–15, emphasises the significance of tear-stains as the trademark of Ovid's earlier work, the *Heroides*.
[19] Ovid's exile is not referred to in other sources. See Williams (1994), Ch. 1.

in these two collections are concerned with the miseries of life on the Black Sea. As recent studies have emphasised, Ovid's accounts of Tomis need to be seen in the context of a literary tradition of ethnography and topographic description.[20] Though Ovid has seen Tomis with his own eyes, yet he draws on (among other texts) the description of Scythia in Virgil's *Georgics* (3.339–83) to convey its characteristics. In Virgil, Scythia and Libya play the part of climatic and cultural extremes to the Roman centre. For Ovid on the edge of the empire, Rome becomes rather the polar antithesis of barbarian Tomis. In some ways the most significant feature of Tomis in Ovid's work is that it is not Rome.[21] Yet the polarity between Tomis and Rome affects not only the description of Tomis but also that of Rome itself, as we shall see below.

Ovid's relationship to Rome, as figured in the exile poems, is also intimately connected with some central concerns of his earlier work. Especially in *Tristia* I, where Ovid treats his departure from Rome, the city has a central place. The first line of the first poem ends with the word *urbem*.

Parve – nec invideo – sine me, liber, ibis in urbem,
    ei mihi, quo domino non licet ire tuo!

Little book, you will go without me – I don't begrudge you –
to the city, from which your poor master is forbidden.

(*Tristia* I.I.I–2)

Just as in the *Amores* Ovid's book might go where the lover dared not – into the house of his mistress – so too now a book, unlike the banished poet, may make its way to Rome.[22] The opening lines of the collection, then, establish Ovid's absence from Rome, as well as the city's importance as intended audience for his poems. At the same time, they remind the reader of Ovid's earlier elegiac work, the *Amores* and the *Heroides* (verse epistles from mythological heroines, dominated by themes of separation, loss and betrayal). Though the exile poems have sometimes been seen as

[20] On Ovid's representation of Tomis see Videau-Delibes (1991), 107–78; Williams (1994), 7–49. On the literary tradition of representing different places and peoples, see Thomas (1982).

[21] Cf. Videau-Delibes (1991), 107.

[22] Cf. e.g. *Amores* 3.8.6: *quo licuit libris non licet ire mihi* (also 2.15.9 and *Her.* 18.15–16). For Hinds (1985), 13–14, the emphasis in the opening lines on the book's freedom (in contrast to the poet's confinement) suggests a pun on *liber* 'book' and *liber* 'free'.

sincere and unadorned expressions of feeling from the previously artful and allusive Ovid, the opening of the first poem makes clear that Ovid's metamorphosis is in some ways less drastic than he himself claims.[23]

The suffering lover of the *Amores*, Ovid's first extant work, and the banished poet of the exile poems, his last, are curiously similar, as scholars have noted. The exile experiences symptoms commonly observed in the lovesick: thinness, pallor, inability to sleep.[24] A number of poems in the *Amores* play on the topos of the *exclusus amator*, familiar from earlier love poetry: the lover, outside his mistress's door, begs to be let in, addressing sometimes the mistress, sometimes the door-keeper, sometimes the door itself. As Ovid begs to be allowed into Rome, his portrayal of the *poeta relegatus* redeploys this topos to more serious ends.[25] Nagle suggests that the relationship between Ovid and Augustus should be seen as parallel to that between the poet and his mistress in the love elegies of Propertius. Certainly it is the emperor who plays the role of the cruel mistress in excluding the poet.[26] But it is not the emperor who functions as the object of the poet's desire. This part, indeed, is sometimes played by the poet's wife but sometimes too by the city of Rome itself.[27]

Wife and city are often paired in the exile poems as the things most missed by Ovid, the elision of absent city and absent woman serving to imply a feminine personification of Rome.[28] The city, of course, has a prominent part in Ovid's love poetry. The *Amores* and the *Ars amatoria* are set among the colonnades, temples and open spaces of Augustan Rome. There is nothing pastoral about Ovid's urbane Cupid; Rome as the city of love is pervasive in his writings.[29] From being the setting for love in Ovid's earlier work, Rome, now absent in his exile poetry, moves into the foreground to become an object of desire in itself. As we shall see below, later readers of Ovid's poetry, who came to Rome as foreigners, drew on his elegiac poems to present Rome as the city of erotic discovery and as itself an object of erotic desire.

[23] On the disingenuousness of Ovid's exile poetry see Nagle (1980), Hinds (1985), Williams (1994).
[24] E.g. *Tristia* 3.8; 4.6; *Pont.* 1.10. Cf. Nagle (1980), 21–2, 43–69.
[25] Nagle (1980), 21–2, 56–62.
[26] Though Ovid does not use the vocabulary of amatory reproach in addressing the emperor (cf. Nagle (1980), 63).
[27] Ovid's wife is figured as beloved (cf. Nagle (1980), 43–55).
[28] E.g. *Tristia* 3.4b.53–4; 3.8.7–8; 3.11.15–16; 4.3.7–8; 5.1.39.
[29] Cf. Labate (1984), 37–64.

In the first poem of the *Tristia*, Ovid's book, sent as an emissary to plead the poet's cause, is also presented as an indirect means for the poet to revisit the city.[30] Though appearing in the first line of the poem, the city is not named until l. 57, when Ovid repeats his directions for the book. The book is to represent its author:

> tu tamen, tu pro me, tu cui licet, aspice Romam.
>   di facerent, possem nunc meus esse liber!
> nec te, quod venias magnam peregrinus in urbem,
>   ignotum populo posse venire puta.
> ut titulo careas, ipso noscere colore;
>   dissimulare velis, te liquet esse meum.

> You, though, go in my place, you go, to whom it is permitted, and set eyes on Rome. If only the gods could let me now be my book! And do not think, because you come as a stranger to a great city, that you can remain unknown to the people. Though you may lack a title, you'll be known by your very complexion. You may try to hide it but you're clearly one of mine.   (57–62)

The book will be recognised, yet it will still be a stranger in the city – just as its author is a stranger in Tomis. The book visits the Palatine, then finally Ovid's own home.[31] Ovid's poems are now the only means through which he can maintain a presence in the city.[32] They function as the exile's children, as his name, even as his body – as well, of course, of allowing him, through a familiar pun, the only feet he is permitted to use in Rome (1.1.16).[33]

Tristia 3.1 echoes the first poem of Book 1. This time it is not the poet who speaks but his book: *Missus in hanc venio timide liber exulis urbem*, 'Sent to this city, I come timidly, the book of an exile.' Already described as *peregrinus* in *Tristia* 1.1, now *hospes in urbe*, 'a stranger in the city' (20),

---

[30] The motif of book as emissary to Rome was later taken up by Martial, writing from Spain, 3.4, 12.2.

[31] The lines describing the book's arrival in Ovid's house are analysed by Hinds (1985), 17–21.

[32] Cf. e.g. *Tristia* 3.10.1–2; 5.4. Even Ovid's poems, however, are not completely free. Cf. *Tristia* 3.1.65–72; *Pont.* 1.1 (poems excluded from public libraries).

[33] Davisson discusses Ovid's representation of his books as his children (1984). This idea is developed further by Hinds, who explores the notion of Ovid's books as parricides (1985), 17–20.

the semi-barbarous book lacks the degree of polish, indeed the command
of Latin, readers would expect from the stylus of Ovid – or so we are
told.[34] Hesitantly, *lingua titubante* (21), the book asks the way. At last he
finds a guide who shows him the Forum of Caesar, the Via Sacra, the
temple of Vesta, the site of Numa's palace, the temple of Jupiter Stator.
The book's itinerary follows closely that of Aeneas and his guide
Evander in *Aeneid* 8. Like Evander's tour, it culminates on the Palatine,
where the book catches sight of Augustus' house.

The book gazes with provincial astonishment at the ruler's residence,
its entrance marked by oak wreath and laurel.

> singula dum miror, video fulgentibus armis
>   conspicuos postes tectaque digna deo
> et 'Iovis haec' dixi 'domus est?' quod ut esse putarem
>   augurium menti querna corona dabat.

> Just as I was marvelling at all these things, I saw an entrance
> distinguished by gleaming weaponry, a residence fit for a god
> and I asked, 'Is this the home of Jupiter?' It was the oak
> wreath that made me think it.   (3.1.33–6)

The book goes on to emphasise the symbolic significance of the oak
(awarded for saving citizens) and the laurel (associated with victory and
specifically with Apollo the god of Actium).[35] This apparently naive
admiration is, however, undercut by an echo of Virgil *Aeneid* 8: on the
same Palatine hill, Evander invites Aeneas into his humble cottage,
telling him that he should spurn wealth, for even Hercules did not spurn
Evander's poor abode (this passage is quoted in Chapter 1 above).
Though not so very grand by some standards (Suetonius, writing in the
second century, noted the modest decor of Augustus' house, *Aug.* 72), the
ruler's glittering residence in Ovid's *Tristia* scarcely conforms to Evander's
prescription. Ovid's ironic reading of Virgil problematises what might
otherwise be read as deferential homage to Augustus, thereby calling into
question a number of other passages in the exile poems which might seem
fulsome compliments to the princeps.

[34] On the importance of *cultus*, see *Ars am.* 3.101–28.
[35] For a discussion of Augustus' house as it appears in this passage see Wiseman
    (1987), esp. 403–5. For another Ovidian account of the approach to Augustus'
    residence – this time as model for Olympus – see *Met.* 1.168–76.

Virgil's *Aeneid* is also evoked in the third poem of *Tristia*.[36] The poet looks back to his final night in Rome.

> Cum subit illius tristissima noctis imago,
> > quod mihi supremum tempus in urbe fuit,
> cum repeto noctem, qua tot mihi cara reliqui,
> > labitur ex oculis nunc quoque gutta meis.

> When comes to me the wretched vision of that night, my last
> few hours in Rome, when I go back to that night, when I left
> so many things that were dear to me, even now a tear rolls
> from my eyes.   (*Tristia* 1.3.1–4)

A parallel between Ovid's last night in Rome and Aeneas' last night in Troy is explicitly offered later at l.26. Already the opening of Ovid's poem suggests similarities. As in *Aeneid* 2, the pain of departure is recalled rather than directly narrated. The poet of the *Tristia*, like Aeneas, weeps in remembering his last night in his native city. The first line of *Tristia* 1.3, *subit illius . . . noctis imago* echoes *subiit cari genitoris imago*, 'the image of my dear father rose up before me' (*Aen.* 2.560). Later details also echo the *Aeneid*. Just as Aeneas picks up his shield, *clipeus*, preparing to avenge the death of Priam (2.671), so Ovid presents himself as taking up his shield to fight (1.3.35–6). Finally, the speech made by Ovid's wife, wanting to accompany her husband, as an expression of *pietas* (1.3.81–6) evokes the speech of Creusa, the wife Aeneas leaves behind (675–8).

Ovid, the elegiac poet who spurned warfare for the life of love, has finally been turned into an epic hero in spite of himself. The exile poems repeatedly set up and explore parallels between Ovid and epic heroes.[37] The poet of the *Tristia* (1.5.57–80) claims, for instance, he is more to be pitied than Ulysses, for not only was battle-hardened Ulysses ultimately bound for home but also his troubles were fictitious (a comment to make the experienced reader of Ovid pause). Ovid's identification with Aeneas in *Tristia* 1.3 is perhaps more pointed. Aeneas, ancestor of the Julii and proto-founder of Rome, was deployed extensively in Augustan visual imagery, as well as literature. The *Aeneid* by the time Ovid left the city was well established as the pre-eminent poem of Augustan Rome and

---

[36] Parallels are suggestively explored by Videau-Delibes (1991), 29–49.
[37] An idea which recurs at *Tristia* 1.2; 3.2.

many readers must have seen a resemblance between its eponymous hero and the emperor Augustus.[38] In daring to compare 'small with great' by figuring himself as Aeneas, Ovid invites his readers to compare the circumstances of his own departure from Rome with those of Aeneas' departure from Troy. Ovid, like Aeneas, is forced by divine will, in Ovid's case the will of Augustus, to leave his native city. But there are significant differences: Rome, unlike Troy, is not at war. While Aeneas, first fighting, then fleeing, was surrounded by the chaos and turmoil of battle, Rome is at peace – the silence is emphasised (1.3.27–8); the epic drama of Ovid's departure seems perhaps incongruous. Might not the ends to which Augustus deploys his divine anger seem by contrast trivial? Aeneas' journey, his epic suffering, is part of a divine plan for the foundation of Rome. Though he leaves Troy, he goes to found a new Troy in Rome (some aspects of the complex relationship between Rome and Troy were discussed in Chapter 2 below). Ovid's journey is a reverse of that of Aeneas' – undoing the work of founding Rome.

Many poems in the *Tristia* and the *Ex Ponto* emphasise the divine and irresistible power of the emperor. Yet the real extent of Augustus' power is called into question in a number of ways in the exile poems. Ovid's destination, though far from the city, still lies within the Roman empire. The city of Rome and the Roman empire are often identified in Augustan literature, as we saw in Chapter 4. The final hexameter of the first poem in the *Tristia* ends with *orbis*, balancing *urbem* in the first line. Here, however, *urbs* and *orbis* are not conflated but contrasted. Ovid makes clear repeatedly that this part of the empire bears little trace of Rome; indeed, it can be described as Rome's antithesis. Wild and war-torn, Tomis lies at the edge of Rome's domain, where the *pax Augusta*, so lavishly celebrated back in Rome, is meaningless.

> vix hac invenies totum, mihi crede, per orbem,
>   quae minus Augusta pace fruatur humus.

> Believe me, even if you searched the whole world, you'd hardly be able to find any place enjoying so little of the Augustan peace.   (*Ex Ponto* 2.5.17–18)

---

[38] On the increasing deployment of the figure of Aeneas see Evans (1992), 42–54; Gruen (1993), 6–51.

Similarly *Tristia* 2 comments on the constant dangers besetting this region of the empire from enemies supposedly conquered many years previously by the Augustan legions (2.189–94).[39]

The almost unrelieved horrors of barbarian Tomis are offset by elegant charms of civilised Rome. Ovid several times describes himself as carried away by vivid images of the city:

> aque domo rursus pulchrae loca vertor ad urbis,
>> cunctaque mens oculis pervidet usa suis.
> nunc fora, nunc aedes, nunc marmore tecta theatra,
>> nunc subit aequata porticus omnis humo.
> gramina nunc Campi pulchros spectantis in hortos,
>> stagna et euripi Virgineusque liquor.

> From my home, I turn my steps once more towards the beautiful city's regions and my mind surveys all those places using its own eyes. Now the fora, now the temples, now the theatres clad in marble, now the colonnades and their level grounds rise up before me, and now the grassy Campus Martius with its view of fair gardens, and the pools and canals and the water of the Virgo.   (*Ex Ponto* 1.8.33–8)[40]

The city of gleaming marble, green grass and clear water embodies civilisation: the fora provide space for public business, the temples attest to Rome's proper respect for the gods, the theatres entertain, the Campus Martius offers scope for relaxation and exercise. This is the Rome built by Augustus (with Agrippa). This is the golden, civilised city celebrated in the somewhat problematic context of Ovid's *Ars amatoria* (3.101–28) – the didactic poem on love which seems to have offended Augustus, the champion of morality. In the exile poetry such celebrations of the city serve to highlight the barbaric ruggedness of Tomis. They may also cause the reader to wonder what advantage Augustus gained in banishing from his city the poet who praised it most effectively.

Elsewhere, Ovid focuses rather on the effort needed to summon up images of Rome in the distant hostile Tomitan wasteland. The power of his imagination is such, he writes, that it can, if only for a brief moment, overcome exile and transport the poet back to Rome. Several poems present pictures of imagined public events, triumphs and consular

[39] Cf. Wiedemann (1975).   [40] Cf. Williams (1994), 26–48.

inaugurations, which apparently celebrate Roman supremacy and order, yet also serve to proclaim Ovid's power to defy exile.[41] A triumph over the Germans is imagined in *Tristia* 4.2:

> haec ego summotus qua possum mente videbo:
>   erepti nobis ius habet illa loci:
> illa per immensas spatiatur libera terras,
>   in caelum celeri pervenit illa fuga;
> illa meos oculos mediam deducit in urbem,
>   immunes tanti nec sinit esse boni;
> invenietque animus, qua currus spectet eburnos;
>   sic certe in patria per breve tempus ero.

These things I shall see, though far away, in my mind's eye – the only way I can. My mind still has the right to the place from which I am cut off. Free, it travels through measureless lands. Heaven it reaches in its swift flight and guides my eyes to the centre of the city, not allowing them to miss so great a good. And my mind shall find a way to look upon the ivory chariot. Thus truly for a brief moment I shall be in my native land.   (*Tristia* 4.2.57–64)

With some implausibility, the author of *Amores* 1.2 (celebrating the triumph of Cupid) and *Ars amatoria* 1 (in which triumphs are recommended as offering opportunities to impress potential sexual partners) presents himself as a deferential spectator at the latest triumphal procession. Here too, of course, the emperor is implicitly reproached for banishing one who could have served his regime so well. Yet there is also something transgressive in Ovid's insistence that even exile cannot keep him out of Rome. Caesar has no jurisdiction over the poet's *mens*, as he emphasises at *Tristia* 3.7.48. Indeed it is precisely the continuing imperial power of Rome which guarantees Ovid's survival through his writings: *dumque suis victrix septem de montibus orbem | prospiciet domitum Martia Roma, legar,* 'So long as Mars' Rome looks out from the seven hills over the vanquished world, I shall be read' (3.7.51–2).

---

[41] In the *Ex Ponto* collection, poem 2.1 celebrates the triumph held to mark Germanicus' successes over the Germans, while 4.5 and 4.9 imagine the inauguration as consuls of two of Ovid's friends. For evocations of Rome not connected with public events, see e.g. *Tristia* 3.4.53–62; 3.12.17–26.

In an earlier poem, Ovid dreams that at least his ashes might return to Italy and be buried close to the city (*Tristia* 3.3.65–70). Only thus will the poet's shade be saved, after his death, from wandering perpetually as a stranger amid the barbarians: *perque feros manes hospita semper erit* (64). The *Tristia* and the *Ex Ponto* often present exile itself as equivalent to death.[42] The grieving on Ovid's last night in Rome is compared to mourning at a funeral (*Tristia* 1.3.89–98). Tomis, as described in Ovid's exile poetry, shares many characteristics with the underworld, a barren, frozen wilderness, profoundly *inamabilis*, 'unlovable', an uncommon word which occurs in Virgil only in relation to the underworld.[43]

In contrast, the Rome conjured up in Ovid's exile poetry is heaven on earth. Ovid's book, as we saw, mistook the house of Augustus for the residence of Jupiter (*Tristia* 3.1). Some buildings in Rome, such as Augustus' house and (discussed in the Introduction above) Augustan temples and porticos, are deployed to somewhat ironical ends in the *Tristia*; even in exile Ovid shows he can appropriate the city of Augustus. Yet it is nevertheless an idealised city. If Tomis is the underworld, a land reminiscent of the iron age, then Rome becomes the golden city, the home of the gods.[44]

Alien city

Exile from Rome takes on a very different poetical form in Juvenal's third Satire. This poem comprises a long speech by a character called Umbricius, preceded by some scene-setting, in which the satirist explains that Umbricius is leaving Rome to live in the countryside. The satirist sympathises with Umbricius' despair at urban life, listing some of its most conspicuous hazards. Their encounter takes place on the edge of the city, by the Capuan gate, in a place remembered by Romans as the Grove of Egeria, a nymph who was said to have given advice to Numa, the second of Rome's kings.

The location itself, as described by the satirist, appears to sum up all that is wrong with Rome. This important part of the city's historical landscape has, like so many others in the satirist's view, been taken over

[42] Nagle (1980), 23–35.
[43] Cf. Williams (1994), 11–13.
[44] For Tomis as bearing characteristics of the iron age, see Williams (1994), 14–15. For Rome as home of the gods, see *Tristia* 1.5.70.

by foreigners, in this case Jews. The pristine appearance of the grove has
been spoilt. The grotto has become:

> dissimilis veris. quanto praesentius esset
> numen aquis, viridi si margine cluderet undas
> herba nec ingenuum violarent marmora tofum.

> a fake. How much closer the divine spirit would feel, if the
> water was surrounded by a grassy bank and the native tufa
> was innocent of marble!   (3.18–20)

Here, as in the rest of Rome, artifice reigns. The nymph's sacred pool is
no longer surrounded by Italian limestone and green grass but by
imported marble – a local material and semi-rustic setting have given way
to inappropriate and foreign decoration.

Umbricius' catalogue of complaint about life in the city covers the
difficulty of earning a living (unless you're Greek), the lack of respect for
any but the rich, the physical discomforts and dangers which beset the life
of the impoverished city-dweller and finally the contrasting charms of life
in the country. To some extent, these complaints are part of the
traditional rhetorical vocabulary of attacks on life in the city and praise
for life in the country.[45] The extent of foreign influence within the city is a
regular feature in moralistic Roman contrasts between city and country.
Varro, for instance, complains about Romans wasting their time in the
Graecorum urbana ... gymnasia, 'citified gymnasia of the Greeks' (*Rust.*
2.pr.2). Umbricius is made to spend lines 59 to 125 in an attack on foreign
habits and foreigners in Rome: *non possum ferre, Quirites,* | *Graecam
urbem*, 'O citizens of Rome, I cannot bear the city to be Greek!' (3.60–1).
Romans are chastised for having abandoned the simplicity of their
traditional customs. Greeks are attacked for the flattery and dissimulation
which rapidly endear them to wealthy patrons, at the expense of
genuinely Roman clients. Rome has so far been taken over by Greeks
(and things Greek) that: *non est Romano cuiquam locus hic*, 'There's no
place here for anyone who's Roman' (3.119).

Umbricius has been made an alien not by being transported to an
unfamiliar location but by the transformation of Rome itself.[46] He has

---

[45] A standard topic among themes debated by Roman schoolboys (Quintilian 2.4.24).
Cf. Braund (1989).

[46] Cf. Anderson (1957) and (1984).

become an exile in his own city. His predicament might prompt the reader to think of Rome's most famous exiled poet. Although Ovid has nothing but praise for a Rome of gleaming marble and verdant open spaces and Juvenal nothing but disgust for a Rome of dirt, danger and crowds, there is a curious similarity between the cities they describe. Ovid celebrates Rome as the locus of poetic composition, the home territory of civilised *artes*.[47] In Juvenal's satire, poetry is listed, bathetically, as one of the omnipresent dangers threatening the city dweller, along with fire, collapsing buildings and robbery. The satirist complains that there is no longer any room in the city for *artibus . . . honestis*, 'honest skills' (3.21). Ovid's poetry might be taken to symbolise the very opposite of *artes honestae*; the arts he celebrates in his love poetry, particularly the *Ars amatoria*, are those of dissimulation and seduction. Ovid's writing takes pleasure in the transformation of Rome from a small rustic community into a glittering metropolis, resplendent with exotic marble; Juvenal's satirist, as we have seen, disapproves of marble, while, for Umbricius, endless building work brings only additional inconvenience and danger to the citizen (3.257–61). There is a case, I would suggest, for seeing the idealised longing for Rome of Ovid's exile poetry as the specific object of savage parody in Juvenal's negative representation of the city.

Ovid explicitly compared himself, on the night he left Rome, with Aeneas leaving Troy. Juvenal does not mention Aeneas directly but Umbricius' description of the horrors of Rome includes many features traditionally associated with a city at the mercy of invaders. Indeed Umbricius' Rome has, like Troy, been invaded by Greeks. Like any city under such circumstances it is fraught with danger – buildings collapse, fires ravage people's homes, possessions are looted, women and children, even grandmothers, are at the mercy of the invader's lusts. Ucalegon in line 199 clearly echoes Ucalegon in *Aeneid* 2.312.[48] Umbricius, then, is to be a new Aeneas. He has given up the unequal struggle against the occupier. The embodiment of Roman values, he is now forced to look for a new home.

Yet Umbricius' role as hero is compromised in numerous ways, as is his vision of the good life and his depiction of un-Roman Rome. The image of early Rome offered at the start of the poem is not perhaps so

[47] On Ovid's association of Rome with *artes* see Videau-Delibes (1991), 151–6.
[48] Cf. Fredericks (1973), 65.

unambiguously virtuous as it at first appears. Advice, it is implied, was not all that king Numa received from Egeria: *nocturnae Numa constituebat amicae*, 'Numa used to meet up with his night-time girlfriend' (3.12). *Constituebat*, Courtney suggests, implies 'furtive assignations', while *nocturna amica* has overtones of prostitution.[49] The life Umbricius now looks forward to is hardly straightforwardly Roman. He is leaving the vicious city, swarming with foreigners, for the peace and quiet of a small town. But he has chosen not Praeneste, nor Gabii, nor Tivoli, nor Volsinii, praised earlier in the poem (190–2) as exemplars of the traditional Roman way of life, but rather Cumae. Cumae, in the Bay of Naples, was the oldest Greek colony in Italy – very much a *Graeca urbs*. Moreover the satirist emphasises its closeness to Baiae (3.4), a seaside resort notorious for its association with the luxurious and cosmopolitan Roman elite.[50] The life Umbricius envisages has distinctly Greek connotations, his very name evoking the Epicurean pursuit of philosophical retirement, while his vegetable plot, he boasts, will be able to feed a hundred Pythagorases – another reference, and one embodying both modesty and excess, to the life of decidedly self-conscious simplicity advocated by Greek philosophers (3.223–31).

The contrast between vicious city and virtuous countryside, as well as that between corrupt contemporary Rome and pure early Rome, is subtly compromised in Juvenal's poem. Greek influence, it seems, is inescapable, whether in the city itself or in attempts to escape its excesses. From one perspective the unadulteratedly Roman life of the days of the kings and early republic has disappeared irretrievably. But is it after all rustic simplicity which constitutes the genuinely Roman life? In the end, perhaps, as Ovid implies, what is distinctively Roman is rather the city's thoroughgoing cosmopolitanism. Rome's power is marked by its position as a centre of cultural exchange. Satire, that most capacious of genres – and the only one claimed as genuinely Roman – in its overflowing multifariousness, in its irrepressible excesses, figures for Rome itself.[51] The satirist, moralist par excellence, insistent critic of the Rome he, unlike Umbricius, cannot bear to leave, is for ever *hospes in urbe*, an alien

---

[49] Courtney (1980), *ad loc.*
[50] Cf. Gold (1995), 2. I am grateful to Barbara Gold for allowing me to see her paper in advance of publication.
[51] On the Romanness of satire see Quintilian *Inst.* 10.1.93–5. On the capaciousness and multifariousness of satire as a figure for Roman culture, see Gowers (1993), 124–6.

in the immoral environment of the city, yet central to the city's self-definition.

The longing for Rome of Ovid's exile poetry is inverted in Juvenal to convey a very different kind of alienation from the city. Both these works are profoundly concerned with what it is to be a Roman, with what it is to be an exile. In both the ambiguous figure of Aeneas, the man who must become an exile in order to become a Roman, serves as a model. The final section of this chapter will look at a number of later travellers who left their own countries to come to Rome, exiles in a sense but also drawn by the desire to realise their own identity as Romans.

Exiles in space and time

Ammianus Marcellinus, a Greek intimately familiar with the Latin literary tradition, who came to Rome for the first time in the late fourth century, was profoundly disappointed by the gulf between his expectations of the city and its reality.[52] Celebrated as the ultimate seat of a virtue which guaranteed imperial power in the books through which Ammianus had first come to know Rome, the city seemed to him rather a sink of vice and luxury (14.6).[53] Rome has often been a disappointment. Montaigne claimed in his travel journal he could not recognise the Rome he knew from literature in the Rome he visited. Nor would the ancient Romans have recognised their city, he suggests.[54]

Rome itself may seem to those who know it first through books disconcertingly strange or strangely familiar. Goethe arrived in Rome for the first time in 1786 aged 37. His travel memoirs, composed many decades later but based on his writings of the time, present his response as follows:

> All the dreams of my youth have come to life; the first engravings I remember – my father hung views of Rome in the hall – I now see in reality, and everything I have known for so long through paintings, drawings, etchings, woodcuts, plastercasts and cork models is now

[52] See Matthews (1989), 12–13.
[53] Though the contrast between Rome's virtuous past and decadent present was a topos of Roman literature of the late republic and early principate also. Cf. Edwards (1993), 6–7, 42–7.
[54] Montaigne (1958), 943–4.

assembled before me. Wherever I walk I come upon familiar objects in an unfamiliar world; everything is just as I imagined it, yet everything is new.[55]

Goethe's representation of his longing to see Rome (such was his anticipation, he claims, that he could not bear to stop longer than a couple of hours in Florence on the way) has much in common with the feelings expressed by Petrarch, Gibbon and Freud (whose responses were examined briefly in the Introduction to this book). All four finally arrived in Rome after years of reading about it. For these, as for many other visitors, longing for the not-yet-visited Rome mirrors the longing for lost Rome expressed by exiled Romans – in literature which will have been very familiar to some at least of these later visitors.

Rome, unlike, for instance, Athens, had always offered the possibility of becoming Roman. Petrarch, as we saw earlier, was made a Roman citizen in a fourteenth-century ceremony which sought to revive the traditions of antiquity. Montaigne, in the sixteenth century, attained Roman citizenship with the support of the pope.[56] In the 1870s, the German scholar Ferdinand Gregorovius, author of a magisterial history of medieval Rome, was rewarded for his labours with Roman citizenship. He was the first Protestant to receive this honour.[57] Profoundly immersed in the literature of Rome, Gregorovius expresses his feelings on leaving the city in terms influenced by Cicero (as well as by Gibbon, another great Protestant historian of the eternal city). In his *Roman Journal*, Gregorovius writes: 'On coming down from the Capitol yesterday, it seemed as if buildings, monuments and stones called me aloud by name.'[58] Thus personifying Rome in the manner of Cicero might a Protestant German from East Prussia show himself a true Roman.

Ancient personifications of Rome, as we have seen, present the city in female form. Ovid's exile poetry elides wife and city as the lost object of love. Martial, a few decades later, compares his beloved to the city. Despite her Spanish origins, her refined sweetness might be taken for Roman, he writes. Indeed, *tu desiderium dominae mihi mitius urbis | esse iubes: Romam tu mihi sola facis*, 'You command my desire for my

[55] Goethe (1962), 129.
[56] Montaigne (1958), 962.
[57] The award of Roman citizenship by the city government was no doubt partly intended to annoy the Church.
[58] Gregorovius (1911), 458

mistress city to abate. By yourself you make a Rome for me' (12.21.9–10). Later visitors to Rome develop this idea of Rome as woman. Du Bellay, in the sixteenth century, characterises Rome as a seductive mistress, drawing him away from his legitimate wife, France.[59] For many young aristocratic visitors to Rome in modern times a stay in Rome offered the opportunity to discover love – or at least sex.[60] Goethe, who seems to have had his first sexual experience in Rome, subsequently created a sequence of poems, *Roman Elegies*, in which Rome functions as the setting for a series of Ovidian erotic encounters.[61] The first of these elegies concludes with the words: 'O Rome, though you are a whole world, yet without love the world would not be the world, nor would Rome be Rome.' To become fully Roman is once again a question of knowledge, this time carnal. Sexual consummation functions as a powerful metaphor for intellectual, spiritual and emotional intimacy with the city.

Madame de Staël's *Corinne*, first published in 1807, a novel which at once became required reading for all educated visitors to Rome, presents as its principal character a woman who may be interpreted as standing for Rome itself (even though she is not as Italian as she seems at first).[62] The eponymous heroine of *Corinne* (the name of Ovid's fictive mistress in his *Amores*, as well as of a Greek woman poet) is spontaneous and passionate – qualities regularly attributed to Italians by northern visitors. She is also intimately familiar with Rome's monuments, pagan and Christian, and shares her knowledge with the British aristocrat Lord Nelvil. Nelvil simultaneously comes to know both woman and city. In the end, however, he cannot commit himself to either, for he is distracted by a sense of his responsibilities back home and by a suspicion that Corinne and respectable northern domestic life might not be altogether compatible. Becoming fully Roman might involve an exile too costly for some.

Goethe, at the very end of his *Italian Journey*, describes his last nights in Rome.

After having walked along the Corso – perhaps for the last time – I walked up to the Capitol, which rose like an enchanted palace in a

---

[59] Ferguson (1984), 29–30.
[60] Eustace warns his readers against vice (1821), 1 66–9.
[61] Boyle (1991), 571–641.
[62] Numerous passages from *Corinne* are quoted in Augustus Hare's *Walks in Rome* first published 1871. Cf. Buzard (1993), 134.

desert . . . I walked down by the stairs at the back. There I was suddenly confronted by the dark triumphal arch of Septimius Severus, which cast a still darker shadow. In the solitude of the Via Sacra, the well-known objects seemed alien and ghost-like. But when I approached the grand ruins of the Colosseum and looked through the gate into the interior, I must frankly confess that a shudder ran through me and I quickly returned home . . . I drew up a *summa summarum* of my whole stay in Italy, and this aroused in my agitated soul a mood I might call heroic-elegiac, for it tried to embody itself in the poetic form of an elegy. At such a moment, how could I fail to remember the elegy of Ovid, the poet who also was exiled and forced to leave Rome on a moonlit night? *Cum repeto noctem.* I could not get him out of my head, with his homesick memories, his sadness and misery far away on the Black Sea . . .[63]

Goethe's journal ends with his own attempt at a farewell elegy to Rome, followed by, finally, lines 1–4 and 27–34 of *Tristia* I.3.

> iamque quiescebant voces hominumque canumque,
>   Lunaque nocturnos alta regebat equos.
> hanc ego suspiciens ad hanc Capitolia cernens
>   quae nostro frustra iuncta fuere Lari,
> 'numina vicinis habitantia sedibus,' inquam,
>   'iamque oculis numquam templa videnda meis,
> dique relinquendi, quos urbs habet alta Quirini,
>   este salutati tempus in omne mihi . . .'

> And then the voices of men and of dogs were quiet and high above the Moon drove her horses of the night. Looking up at her and by her light seeing the Capitol, which to no purpose stood beside our home, I said, 'O deities who dwell close by, and temples I shall never see again, and gods held by the high city of Quirinus, whom I must leave, farewell, I bid you, for ever . . .'   (*Tristia* I.3.27–34)

Thus Goethe, like so many visitors to Rome, comes to figure himself, on leaving, as a Roman compelled to leave his own country. To a greater degree than Ovid in *Tristia* I.3, Goethe focuses on the buildings of Rome.

---

[63] Goethe (1962), 497–8.

Though Ovid's city is silent, his house at least is full of grieving friends and family. There are no human presences in Goethe's Rome. His last walks suggest isolation and alienation – a lone Romantic figure in a desert of ruins.[64] This emptiness sets off his summoning-up of past presences – those of Rome's gods and of the exiled poet.

For the visitor with pressing responsibilities in his own country, there was ultimately only one way to stay on in Rome. Goethe devoted much of his time in Italy to improving his drawing technique; one of his sketches shows a tomb in Rome's picturesque, overgrown Protestant cemetery, in the shadow of the pyramid of Gaius Cestius. The tomb is Goethe's own.[65] Chateaubriand, too, his career as ambassador to Rome truncated in 1829, unhappy at the thought of returning to political life in France, thought longingly of death in Rome: 'Eternal exile among the ruins of Rome had been my dearest dream.'[66] Ovid, longing for Rome from his distant place of exile, characterised exile as death. Later writers, feeling Rome to be home yet also exile, were more ambivalent. Death alone perhaps can assuage the exile's desire for full citizenship in the eternal city.

[64] A similar evocation of deserted Rome occurs in Chateaubriand's 'Promenade dans Rome au clair de la lune', as McGann notes (1984), 84–5.
[65] Cf. Boyle (1991), 508.
[66] (1962), 385.

Epilogue: the transcendent city

Tying ideas and monuments to places may seem to anchor them, to give them permanence. Thus the Capitol could serve to embody Rome's imperial power. Yet, as the very word 'Rome' has often been made to imply, no monument, not even the greatest, can last for ever. The city of Rome was sacked by the Goths in 410 CE. Life in the city was, in practical terms, perhaps not much affected. But in symbolic terms this was a moment of profound rupture.[1] Augustine in North Africa sought to reassure his followers: 'the city is built of citizens not of walls' (*De urbis excidio* VI, 6). Particularity of place, in Augustine's formulation, is no longer significant. Rome need not be in Rome. This was an idea which had been in the time of Lucan a shocking paradox. But in the fifth century, the walls of Rome ceased to offer the comfort of eternity.

Augustine's Christian city, a city without physical location, was termed *civitas* rather than *urbs*. Yet when he sought means to affirm the infinite superiority of divine to secular power, the nearest model he could find for the kingdom of God was the empire of the Romans. Even in antiquity the vast majority of citizens of Rome had no physical connection with the city. Romans need not be born in Rome. In a sense it was this which allowed the idea of Rome to become a concept only partly attached to a particular place.

As Petrarch emphasised, in his attempt to persuade the pope to return there, Rome is both a city of ruins – its walls and palaces have fallen – and also an idea whose glory is immortal. The poignancy of the disjunction

---

[1] On Christian responses to the sack of Rome, see Paschoud (1967), Mazzolani (1970), 242–79.

between Rome's glory and Rome's ruin has been intensified by succeeding generations of literary visitors. Yet it is because the city is in ruins that the idea may be appropriated in the service of new and diverse regimes, that of the Christian church most notably but also those of the Founding Fathers of the United States, of the French revolutionaries – and of the British proconsuls. The notion of 'Rome' has been detached from its material aspect to take on an endlessly mobile symbolic life.

Bibliography

Alföldi, Andreas (1974) *Die Struktur des voretruskischen Römerstaates.* Heidelberg

Alison, Archibald (1790) *Essays on the Nature and Principles of Taste.* Edinburgh

Anderson, W. S. (1957) 'Studies in book I of Juvenal', *YClS* 15: 55–68

    (1984) 'Rustic urbanity: Roman satirists in and out of Rome', *CO* 61.4: 111–17

André, J.-M. and Baslez, M.-F. (1993) *Voyager dans l'antiquité.* Paris

Bakhtin, M.M. (1981) *The Dialogic Imagination* tr. Caryl Emerson and Michael Holquist. Austin

Balland, André (1984) 'La *casa Romuli* au Palatin et au Capitole', *REL* 62: 57–80

Balsdon, J.P.V.D. (1979) *Romans and Aliens.* London

Bann, Stephen (forthcoming) 'Gibbon and Granet in dialogue', in Edwards (forthcoming).

Barchiesi, Alessandro (1994) *Il poeta e il principe: Ovidio e il discorso augusteo.* Rome

Barkan, Leonard (1991) *Transuming Passion: Ganymede and the Erotics of Humanism.* Stanford

Barker, Duncan (1993) 'Gold and the renascence of the Golden Race: a study of the relationship between gold and the "Golden Age" ideology of Augustan Rome', PhD. diss., Cambridge

Beard, Mary (1987) 'A complex of times: no more sheep on Romulus' birthday', *PCPhS* 33: 1–15

    (1994) 'Religion' in *CAH* IX, 2nd edn: 729–68

Boatwright, M.T. (1987) *Hadrian and the City of Rome.* Princeton

Bonjour, Madeleine (1975a) *Terre natale: études sur une composante affective du patriotisme romain.* Paris

    (1975b) 'Les personnages féminins et la terre natale dans l'épisode de Coriolan (Liv., 2.40)', *REL* 53: 157–81

Bourgeaud, P. (1987) 'Du mythe à l'idéologie: la tête du Capitole', *MusHelv* 44: 86–100

Boyle, Nicholas (1991) *Goethe: The Poet and the Age* vol. I. Oxford

Braund, S.H. (1989) 'City and country in Roman satire', 23–47 in Braund ed. *Satire and Society in Ancient Rome.* Exeter

Bréguet, E. (1969) '*Urbi et orbi* : un cliché et un thème', 140–52 in *Hommages à M. Renard* I. Brussels

Brown, Peter (1967) *Augustine of Hippo*. London

Burke, P.F. (1979) 'Roman rites for the dead and *Aeneid* 6', *CJ* 74: 220–8

Buzard, James (1993) *The Beaten Track: European Tourism, Literature and the Ways to Culture 1800–1918*. Oxford

Cameron, Alan (1970) *Poetry and Propaganda at the Court of Honorius*. Oxford

Camps, W.A. ed. (1965) *Propertius Elegies Book IV*. Cambridge

Cancik, Hubert (1985) 'Rome as sacred landscape and the end of republican religion in Rome', *Visible Religion: Annual for Religious Iconography* 4: 250–65

Carettoni, Gianfilippo (1983) *Das Haus des Augustus auf Palatin*. Mainz

Cartledge, Paul (1989) 'The Tacitism of Edward Gibbon (two hundred years on)', *Mediterranean History Review* 4: 251–70

Ceausescu, Petre (1976) '*Altera Roma* : histoire d'une folie politique', *Historia* 25: 79–108

Cederna, Antonio (1980) *Mussolini urbanista*. Rome

Chateaubriand, François René de (1962) *The Memoirs* tr. Robert Baldick. London

Classen, C.J. (1980) *Die Stadt im Spiegel der Descriptiones und Laudes Urbium*. Hildesheim

Coarelli, Filippo (1968) 'La porta trionfale e la via dei trionfi', *DA* 2.1: 55–103

   (1977) 'Public building in Rome between the Second Punic War and Sulla', *PBSR* 45: 1–19

   (1983) *Il Foro Romano I: periodo arcaico*. Rome

   (1985) *Il Foro Romano II: periodo reppublicano e augusteo*. Rome

Colonna, B.G. (1940) 'L'isolamento del Campidoglio: demolizioni e ricordi', *Capitolium* 15: 521–40

Connor, P.J. (1978) 'The Actian miracle: Propertius 4.6', *Ramus* 7: 1–10

Conte, G.B. (1994) *Genres and Readers* tr. Glenn W. Most. Baltimore

Courtney, E. (1980) *A Commentary on the Satires of Juvenal*. London

Craddock, Patricia B. (1984) 'Edward Gibbon and the ruins of the Capitol', in Patterson (1984).

Dahlmann, Hellfried (1976) 'Zu Varros antiquarisch-historischen Werken besonders den *antiquitates rerum humanarum et divinarum*', 163–76 in *Atti congresso internazionale di studi Varroniani* vol. I. Rieti

Davisson, M.H.T. (1984) 'Parents and children in Ovid's poems from exile', *CW* 78: 111–14

De Brohun, J.B. (1994) 'Redressing Elegy's *puella*: Propertius IV and the rhetoric of fashion' *JRS* 84: 41–63

D'Onofrio, Cesare (1989) *Visitiamo Roma nel quattrocento: la città degli umanisti*. Rome

Dupont, Florence (1992) *Daily Life in Ancient Rome* tr. Christopher Woodall. Oxford

Duret, L. and Néraudau, J.P. (1983) *Urbanisme et métamorphoses de la Rome antique*. Paris

Eck, Werner (1984) 'Senatorial self-representation: developments in the Augustan period', 129–67 in Fergus Millar and Erich Segal eds. *Augustus Caesar: Seven Aspects*. Oxford

Edwards, Catharine (1993) *The Politics of Immorality in Ancient Rome*. Cambridge

   ed. (forthcoming) *Palimpsests: Reading Rome 1789–1945*

Elsner, J. (1994) 'Constructing decadence: the representation of Nero as imperial builder', 112–27 in Elsner and Masters (1994).

Elsner, J. and Masters, J. eds. (1994) *Reflections of Nero: Culture, History and Representation*. London

Ernst, Wolfgang (forthcoming) 'Archaeologically correct? Representations of ancient Rome in the novel', in Edwards (forthcoming).

Eustace, John Chetwode (1821) *Classical Tour through Italy*. London (1st edn 1812)

Evans, J.D. (1992) *The Art of Persuasion: Political Propaganda in Rome from Aeneas to Brutus*. Ann Arbor

Fabricius, Georgius (1551) *Roma*. Basel

Favro, Diane (1993) 'Reading the Augustan city', 230–57 in P.J.Holliday ed. *Narrative and Event in Ancient Art*. Cambridge

Feeney, Denis (1986) 'History and revelation in Virgil's underworld', *PCPhS* 32: 1–24
(1991) *The Gods in Epic*. Oxford
(1992) '*Si licet et fas est* : Ovid's *Fasti* and the problem of free speech under the principate', 1–25 in Powell (1982).

Ferguson, Margaret (1984) '"The afflatus of ruin": meditations on Rome by Du Bellay, Spencer and Stevens', 23–50 in Patterson (1984).

Fredericks, S.C. (1973) 'The function of the prologue (1–20) in the organisation of Juvenal's Third Satire' *Phoenix*, 27: 62–7

Freud, Sigmund (1985) *Civilisation, Society and Religion* tr. Albert Dickson. London

Gibbon, Edward (1909–1914) *Decline and Fall of the Roman Empire* ed. J.B.Bury. London
(1897) *The Autobiographies of Edward Gibbon* ed. John Murray. London
(1961) *Gibbon's Journey from Rome to Geneva* ed. G.A. Bonnard. London

Goethe, J.W. (1962) *Italian Journey* tr. W.H. Auden and Elizabeth Mayer. London

Gold, Barbara (1995) 'City life in Juvenal's *Satires*', in *The Shapes of City Life in Rome and Pompeii: Essays in Honor of Lawrence Richardson Jr on the Occasion of his Retirement*. New Rochelle, NY

Goldstein, Laurence (1977) *Ruins and Empire: The Evolution of a Theme in Augustan and Romantic Literature*. Pittsburgh

Gowers, E.J. (1993) *The Loaded Table: Representations of Food in Roman Literature*. Oxford
(1995) 'The anatomy of Rome from Capitol to Cloaca', *JRS* 85: 23–32

Graf, A. (1915) *Roma nella memoria e nelle immaginazioni del medio evo*. Turin

Gransden, K.W. (1976) *Virgil Aeneid Book VIII*. Cambridge

Greene, T.M. (1982) 'Resurrecting Rome: the double task of the humanist imagination', 41–54 in Ramsey (1982).

Gregorovius, Ferdinand (1898) *History of the City of Rome in the Middle Ages* tr. Annie Hamilton. London
(1911) *The Roman Journals of Ferdinand Gregorovius, 1852–1874* tr. A. Hamilton, London (1st German edn 1892)

Griffin, Miriam (1976) *Seneca: A Philosopher in Politics*. Oxford

Gros, Pierre (1976a) *Aurea templa: recherches sur l'architecture religieuse de Rome à l'époque d'Auguste*. Rome

(1976b) 'Les premières générations d'architectes hellénistiques à Rome', 387–410 in *Mélanges Huergon*. Rome

Gruen, E.S. (1993) *Culture and National Identity in Republican Rome*. London

Harada, Jiro (1937) *A Glimpse of Japanese Ideals: Lectures on Japanese Art and Culture*. Tokyo

Hardie, Philip (1991) 'Janus in Ovid's *Fasti*', *MD* 26: 47–64

    (1992) 'Augustan poets and the mutability of Rome', 59–82 in Powell (1982).

    (1993) *The Epic Successors of Virgil: A Study in the Dynamics of a Tradition*. Cambridge

Hare, Augustus (1900) *Walks in Rome*. London (1st edn 1871)

Hellegouarc'h, J. (1970) 'Le principat de Camille', *REL* 48: 112–32

Herbert-Brown, Geraldine (1994) *Ovid and the Fasti*. Oxford

Hinds, Stephen (1985) 'Booking the return trip: Ovid and *Tristia* 1', *PCPhS* 31: 13–32

    (1992) '*Arma* in Ovid's *Fasti*', *Arethusa* 25: 81–153

Hopkins, Keith (1983) *Death and Renewal*. Cambridge

Jaeger, M.K. (1990) 'The poetics of place: the Augustan writers and the urban landscape of Rome', PhD. diss., University of California, Berkeley

    (1993) '*Custodia fidelis memoriae* : Livy's story of M. Manlius Capitolinus', *Latomus* 52: 350–63

Janowitz, Anne (1990) *England's Ruins*. Oxford

Jordan, D.P. (1971) *Gibbon and his Roman Empire*. Urbana

    (1977) 'The historian of the Roman empire', 1–12 in Glen Bowersock, John Clive and S.R.Graubard eds. *Edward Gibbon and the Decline and Fall of the Roman Empire*. Cambridge, Mass.

Keitel, Elizabeth (1984) 'Principate and civil war in the *Annals* of Tacitus', *AJPh* 105: 306–25

Koch, Carl (1960) *Religio: Studien zu Kult und Glauben der Römer*. Nuremberg

Kostof, Spiro (1973) *The Traffic and the Glory: The Third Rome 1870–1950*. Berkeley

Kraft, Konrad (1967) 'Der Sinn des Mausoleums des Augustus', *Historia* 16: 189–206

Kraus, C.S. (1994) '"No second Troy": topoi and refoundation in Livy, Book v', *TAPhA* 124: 267–89

Krautheimer, Richard (1980) *Rome: Profile of a City 312–1308*. Princeton

    (1983) *Three Christian capitals: Topography and Politics, Rome, Constantinople, Milan*. Berkeley

Labate, Mario (1984) *L'arte di farsi amare: modelli culturali e progetto didascalico nell'elegia ovidiana*. Pisa

Lanciani, Rodolfo (1902–12) *Storia degli scavi di Roma e notizie intorno le collezioni romane di antichità*. Rome

Levene, D.S. (1993) *Religion in Livy*. Leiden

Liebeschuetz, W.H.G.L. (1967) 'The religious position of Livy's History', *JRS* 57:45–55

    (1979) *Continuity and Change in Roman Religion*. Oxford

Luce, T.J. (1965) 'The dating of Livy's first decade', *TAPhA* 96: 209–40

    (1990) 'Livy, Augustus and the Forum Augustum', 123–38 in K.Raaflaub and M.Toher eds. *Between Republic and Empire: Interpretations of Augustus and his Principate*. Berkeley

MacDonald, W.L. (1976) *The Pantheon: Design, Meaning and Progeny*. Cambridge, Mass.

McGann, J.J. (1984) 'Rome and its romantic significance', 83–104 in Patterson (1984).

McGowan, Margaret (1994) 'Impaired vision: the experience of Rome in renaissance France', *Renaissance Studies* 8.3: 244–55

Manacorda, D. and Tamassia, R. (1985) *Il piccone del regime*. Rome

Mango, Cyril (1985) *Le développement urbain de Constantinople (IVe–VIIe siècles)*. Paris

Martindale, C.A. (1993) *Redeeming the Text: Latin Poetry and the Hermeneutics of Reception*. Cambridge

(forthcoming) 'Ruins of Rome: Eliot's *Waste Land* and the presence of the past', in Edwards (forthcoming).

Masters, Jamie (1992) *Poetry and Civil War in Lucan's Bellum Civile*. Cambridge

Matthews, John (1986) 'Ammianus and the eternity of Rome', 17–29 in Christopher Holdsworth and T.P.Wiseman eds. *The Inheritance of Historiography 350–900*. Exeter

(1989) *The Roman Empire of Ammianus*. London

Mazzolani, Lidia Storoni (1970) *The Idea of the City in Roman Thought: From Walled City to Spiritual Commonwealth*. London

Mellor, Ronald (1981) 'The goddess Roma', *ANRW* II 17.2: 950–1030

Miglio, Massimo (1982) 'Il leone e la lupa: dal simbolo al pasticcio alla francese', *Studi Romani* 30: 177–86

Miles, Gary B. (1986) 'The cycle of Roman history in Livy's first pentad', *AJPh* 107: 1–33

(1988) '*Maiores, conditores*, and Livy's perspective on the past', *TAPhA* 118: 185–208

Millar, F.G.B. (1986) 'Politics, persuasion and the people before the Social War', *JRS* 76: 1–11

Miller, J.F. (1982) 'Callimachus and the Augustan aetiological elegy', *ANRW* II 30.1: 371–417

Moatti, Claude (1993) *The Search for Ancient Rome*. London

Momigliano, Arnaldo (1941) 'Camillus and Concord', *CQ* 36: 111–20

(1955) 'Ancient history and the antiquarian', 67–106 in *Contributo alla Storia degli Studi Classici*. Rome

(1963) 'Pagan and Christian historiography in the fourth century', 79–99 in Momigliano ed. *The Conflict between Paganism and Christianity in the Fourth Century*. Oxford

(1989) 'The origins of Rome', in *CAH* VII, 2nd edn 52–112

Montaigne, Michel Eyquem de (1958) *The Complete Works of Montaigne* tr. D.M. Frame. London

Nagle, B.R. (1980) *The Poetics of Exile*. Brussels

Nardini, Famiano (1666) *Roma antica*. Rome

New, M. (1978) 'Gibbon, Middleton and the "bare-footed fryars"', *Notes and Queries* 223: 51–2

Nicolet, Claude (1980) *The World of the Citizen in Republican Rome* tr. P.S.Falla. Berkeley

(1991) *Space, Geography and Politics in the Early Roman Empire* tr. Hélène Leclerc. Ann Arbor

O'Brien, Karen (forthcoming) 'Gibbon's prospects: rhetoric, fame and the closing chapters of the *Decline and Fall*, in David Womersley ed. Oxford Voltaire Foundation

Ogilvie, R.M. (1970, 2nd edn) *A Commentary on Livy Books 1–5*. Oxford

Paschoud, F. (1967) *Roma aeterna: études sur le patriotisme romain dans l'occident latin à l'époque des grandes invasions*. Rome

Patterson, Annabel ed. (1984) *Roman Images*. Baltimore

Patterson, J.R. (1992) 'The city of Rome: from republic to empire', *JRS* 82: 186–215

Paul, G.M. (1982) '*Urbs capta* : sketch of an ancient literary motif', *Phoenix* 36: 144–55

Pemble, John (1987) *The Mediterranean Passion: Victorians and Edwardians in the South*. Oxford

Pensabene, Patrizio (1990) 'L'area sud-ovest del Palatino', 86–90 in *La grande Roma dei Tarquini*. Rome

Petrarch, Francesco (1874) *Scritti inediti di Francesco Petrarca* ed. Attilio Hortis. Trieste
    (1975) *Rerum familiarum libri* tr. A.S. Bernardo. Albany

Pinotti, P. (1983) 'Properzio e Vertumno: anticonformismo e restaurazione augustea', 75–96 in *Colloquium Propertianum* III. Assisi

Platner, S.B. and Ashby, T. (1929) *A Topographical Dictionary of Ancient Rome*. Oxford

Poggio Bracciolini, G.F. (1993) *De varietate fortunae* ed. Outi Merisalo. Helsinki

Powell, Anton ed. (1982) *Roman Poetry and Propaganda in the Age of Augustus*. Bristol

Price, S.R.F. (1996) Ch. 4 in Mary Beard, John North and Simon Price eds. *Religions of Rome* I. Cambridge

Purcell, Nicholas (1987) 'Town in country and country in town', 187–203 in E.B. MacDougall ed. *Ancient Roman Villa Gardens*. Dumbarton Oaks
    (1989) 'Rediscovering the Roman Forum', *JRA* 2: 156–66
    (1992) 'The city of Rome', 421–53 in Richard Jenkyns ed. *The Legacy of Rome: A New Appraisal*. Oxford

Ramsey, P.A. ed. (1982) *Rome in the Renaissance: The City and the Myth*. Binghamton

Rawson, Elizabeth (1985) *Intellectual Life in the Late Republic*. London

Richardson, L., Jr (1992) *A New Topographical Dictionary of Ancient Rome*. London

The Life of Cola di Rienzo, tr. with intro. John Wright. Toronto

Romm, J.S. (1992) *The Edges of the Earth in Ancient Thought*. Princeton

Rouveret, Agnès (1991) 'Tacite et les monuments', *ANRW* II 33.4: 3051–99

Rudd, Niall (1976) *Lines of Inquiry*. Cambridge

Saxl, Fritz (1957) 'The Capitol during the renaissance: a symbol of the imperial idea', in *Lectures*. London

Scobie, Alex (1990) *Hitler's State Architecture: The Impact of Classical Antiquity*. Pennsylvania

Serres, Michel (1991) *Rome: The Book of Foundations* tr. F.McCarren. Stanford

Skutsch, O. (1968) *Studia Enniana*. London

Spring, Peter (1972) 'The topographical and archaeological study of the antiquities of the city of Rome 1420–47', PhD. diss., University of Edinburgh

Springer, Carolyn (1987) *The Marble Wilderness: Ruins and Representation in Italian Romanticism 1775–1850*. Cambridge

Stambaugh, John (1988) *The Ancient Roman City*. Baltimore and London

Steinby, E.M. ed. (1993–) *Lexicon Topographicum urbis Romae*. Rome

Stinger, Charles (1985) *The Renaissance in Rome*. Bloomington

Thomas, R.F. (1982) *Lands and Peoples in Roman Poetry: The Ethnographical Tradition*. Cambridge

Trapp, J.B. (1982) 'The poet laureate: Rome, *renovatio* and *translatio imperii*', 93–130 in Ramsey (1982).

Tucker, G.H. (1990) *The Poet's Odyssey: Joachim Du Bellay and the Antiquitez de Rome*. Oxford

Urlichs, C.L. (1871) *Codex urbis Romae topographicus*. Würzburg

Valentini, Roberto and Zucchetti, Giuseppe (1940) *Codice topografico della città di Roma* vol. 1. Rome

Van Deman, E.B. (1922) 'The Sullan forum', *JRS* 12: 1–31

Varriano, John (1991) *Rome: A Literary Companion*. London

Vasaly, Ann (1993) *Representations: Images of the World in Ciceronian Oratory*. Berkeley

Videau-Delibes, Anne (1991) *Les Tristes d'Ovide et l'élégie romaine: une poétique de la rupture*. Paris

Wallace-Hadrill, Andrew (1987) 'Time for Augustus: Ovid, Augustus and the *Fasti*', 221–30 in Michael Whitby, Philip Hardie and Mary Whitby eds. *Homo viator: Classical Essays for John Bramble*. Bristol

(1990) 'Pliny the Elder and man's unnatural history', *G&R* 37.1: 80–96

Weeber, K. (1978) 'Properz 4.1.1–70 und das achte Buch der *Aeneis*', *Latomus* 37: 489–506

Weiss, Roberto (1969) *The Renaissance Discovery of Classical Antiquity*. Oxford

Wiedemann, Thomas (1975) 'The political background to Ovid's *Tristia* 2', *CQ* 25.2: 264–71

Wilkins, E.H. (1955) *Studies in the Life and Work of Petrarch*. Cambridge, Mass.

Williams, Gareth D. (1994) *Banished Voices: Readings in Ovid's Exile Poetry*. Cambridge

Wilton-Ely, John (1978) *The Mind and Art of Giovanni Battista Piranesi*. London

Wiseman, T.P. (1978) 'Flavians on the Capitol', *AJAH* 3: 163–78

(1979) 'Topography and rhetoric: the trial of Manlius', *Historia* 28: 32–50

(1981) 'The temple of Victory on the Palatine', *AJ* 61: 35–52

(1984) 'Cybele, Virgil and Augustus', 117–28 in A.J.Woodman and D.West eds. *Poetry and Politics in the Age of Augustus*. Cambridge

(1986) 'Monuments and the Roman annalists', 87–101 in I.S.Moxon, J.D.Smart and A.J.Woodman eds. *Past Perspectives: Studies in Greek and Roman Historical Writing*. Cambridge

(1987) '*Conspicui postes tectaque digna deo* : the public image of aristocratic and imperial houses in the late republic and early empire', 393–413 in *L'Urbs: espace urbain et histoire*. Collection de l'Ecole Française de Rome 98, Rome

(1995) *Remus: A Roman Myth*. Cambridge.

Womersley, David (1988) *The Transformation of the Decline and Fall of the Roman Empire*. Cambridge

Woodman, A.J. (1988) *Rhetoric in Classical Historiography*. London

Yates, Frances (1966) *The Art of Memory*. London

Zanker, Paul (1968) *Forum Augustum: das Bildprogram*. Tübingen

(1988) *The Power of Images in the Age of Augustus* tr. Alan Shapiro. Ann Arbor

Zetzel, J.E.G. (1989) '*Romane memento* : justice and judgement in *Aeneid* 6', *TAPhA* 119: 263–84

Indexes

GENERAL INDEX

143

INDEX OF PASSAGES DISCUSSED

(Major discussions are indicated by **bold** type.)

Printed in the United States
75246LV00001B/49-66